AN ARTS FOUNDATION COURSE

UNITS 18–19
RELIGION: CONFORMITY AND CONTROVERSY

Prepared by Michael Bartholomew, Stuart Brown, Angus Calder, Briony Fer, Trevor Herbert, Richard Middleton and Gerald Parsons for the Course Team

UNITS 20–21
MORAL VALUES AND THE SOCIAL ORDER

Prepared by Stuart Brown, Briony Fer, Susan Meikle and Gerald Parsons for the Course Team

Cover: 'A city church congregation' from *Illustrated London News*, 5 October 1872.

The Open University
Walton Hall
Milton Keynes
MK7 6AA

First published 1986; second edition 1991

Copyright © 1986 and 1990 The Open University

All rights reserved. No part of this publication may be reproduced, stored in a retrieval system or transmitted in any form or by any means, without written permission from the publisher or a licence from the Copyright Licensing Agency Limited. Details of such licences (for reprographic reproduction) may be obtained from the Copyright Licensing Agency Ltd., 33–34 Alfred Place, London WC1E 7DP.

Designed by the Graphic Design Group of the Open University.

Typeset by Medcalf Type Ltd, Bicester, Oxon
Printed in the United Kingdom by Courier International

ISBN 0 7492 1034 6

This unit forms aprt of an Open University course; a complete list of the units is on the back cover.

If you have not enrolled on the course and would like to buy this or other Open University material, please write to Open University Educational Enterprises, 12 Cofferidge Close, Stony Stratford, Milton Keynes, MK11 1BY, United Kingdom. If you wish to enquire about enrolling as an Open University student, please write to The Open University, PO Box 625, Walton Hall, Milton Keynes, MK1 1TY, United Kingdom.

Units 18–19

RELIGION: CONFORMITY AND CONTROVERSY

1 Introduction	5
2 The varieties of Victorian religion	6
2.1 Anglicanism and Nonconformity	7
2.2 Evangelicalism and Catholicism	8
2.3 Challenges to Victorian religion	15
3 Music in Victorian worship	17
3.1 Historical background	17
3.2 'Hymns Ancient and Modern'	19
3.3 The Oxford Movement	20
3.4 The choral revival	21
3.5 'Popular' choirs and bands	21
3.6 Evangelicals and Nonconformists	22
3.7 Gospel song	23
3.8 Conclusion	25
4 Challenges to orthodoxy from within the church	26
4.1 Either/or: all or nothing	32
4.2 A middle way?	33
5 Challenges to religious authority from scientists and philosophers	35
5.1 The cult of science	35
5.2 The scientists' bid for cultural supremacy	37
5.3 The Prayer Gauge debate	38
5.4 Charles Darwin	41
5.5 The Darwinian debates	43
5.6 The response to Darwin's theory	44
5.7 Conclusion	48
6 Religion and Victorian painting	49
6.1 Pre-Raphaelitism, Ruskin and religious art	49
6.2 Art and religious controversy	54
6.3 Painting, belief and science	55
7 Religion in the poetry of Tennyson and Hopkins	57
References	69

Contributors

Michael Bartholomew wrote the Introduction and section 5. Gerald Parsons wrote sections 2 and 4. Trevor Herbert and Richard Middleton wrote section 3. Briony Fer wrote section 6. Angus Calder wrote section 7. Stuart Brown wrote the paragraphs on Clifford in section 5. Nicola Durbridge contributed to the development of the block as a whole, especially to the exercises. Magnus John helped a great deal with the illustrations.

Units 18–19   Religion: Conformity and Controversy

SET READING

As you work through these units you will need to refer to
Geoffrey Best (1979) *Mid-Victorian Britain 1851–75* (Set Book)
John Golby (ed.) (1986) *Culture and Society in Britain 1850–1890* (Course Reader)
Illustration Booklet
Broadcast Notes
Cassette Notes

BROADCASTING

Television programme 18 *The Victorian High Church*
Television programme 19 *Victorian Dissenting Chapels*
Television programme 20 *Religion and Society in Victorian Bristol*
Television programme 21 *Victorian Views of the Art of the Past*
Radio programme 9 *Hopkins's Religious Poetry*
Radio programme 10 *George Eliot: A Search for Secular Answers*

CASSETTE

Cassette 5, side 1, band 2 *Music in Victorian Worship*

1 INTRODUCTION

The Victorians look familiar to us. We can look at photographs of them in their crinolines, or their top hats, or their rags. We inhabit their towns, travel on their railways, live in their houses, go to their schools, read their novels. The Victorians seem archaic, perhaps, but they are comfortably familiar, inhabiting a world that lies just beyond our grandparents. But the ease of access we have to them conceals huge differences between them and us. And the biggest difference between them and us is that they were religious, and we are not. I do not mean that all Victorians believed and that none of us believes – on the simple test of nominal belief in God, the difference between them and us is only slight. What I mean is that during the nineteenth century, the Christian religion exerted an influence on national life immeasurably more profound than it does today. Religion did more than merely give a flavour, or tone, to Victorian society. It determined and shaped the pattern of that society. It decisively shaped politics – especially local politics – education, science, painting, poetry, music, social class, regional and metropolitan culture. Hardly any area of Victorian life was untouched by it. Even disbelievers could not shake off its influence. If they were intellectuals, they expended great effort in publicly justifying their disbelief. If they were uneducated, and showed no interest in church attendance, they would nevertheless find that their Sundays' activities were subject to religious controls. Religion was simply inescapable, whether it was a body of doctrines requiring intellectual assent or dissent, or a set of institutions that reached out into every aspect of life. But most Victorians, far from wishing to escape from the influence of religion, were either content with it, or positively rejoiced in it.

Units 18–19 examine Victorian religion. We aim to show something of the immense and exotic range of varieties of Christian groups, and to look in detail at religious elements in architecture and church music, evolution theory, Tennyson's and Hopkins's poetry, and Pre-Raphaelite painting. Obviously, we won't cover every aspect of Victorian religion, but we hope that by giving you both the broad outlines, and a sequence of intensive short studies of particular aspects, we will open up for you something of the strangeness and power of Victorian religion.

Scotland, Wales and Ireland each has its own unique and complicated national religious history which, emphatically, is not an appendage to the English story. At the most basic level, it's worth reminding yourself that a Hebridean congregation, an English cathedral congregation and a Welsh chapel congregation spoke and worshipped in quite different languages. And the variation in their doctrine was substantial too. But with just two weeks work ahead of you, it would be impossible to deal adequately with each national tradition. So, with some trepidation, and an awareness of the risk of distortion, we have decided to concentrate chiefly, although not exclusively, on England. But remember, 'England' does not mean 'Britain'.

2 THE VARIETIES OF VICTORIAN RELIGION

For the Victorians, religion was inescapably a part of their lives and of their society and culture in a way that it is not for us. At least in terms of sheer social, political, intellectual and cultural prominence, therefore, Victorian religion exhibited a self-confidence and assurance of a kind not characteristic of religious groups in twentieth-century Britain. The fact that Victorian religion was generally self-confident and self-assured did not mean, however, that it was either *unified* or *unchallenged*. In point of fact it was neither. Victorian religion and religious life was inherently varied, complex and controversial — many of the controversies arising from conflicts between the various religious groups and traditions. Moreover, quite apart from the tensions caused by internal conflict and controversy, Victorian religion was also subject to a number of serious challenges from without, both intellectual and social in origin.

The main aim of this section is to introduce something of the sheer variety and diversity of religion in Victorian Britain. A second aim is to begin to show how the social, intellectual and cultural position and standing of Victorian religion began to be challenged by developments in the period between 1850 and 1890. These latter themes will then be developed in later sections of this part of the course.

You have already encountered some suggestions that Victorian religious life was not all a matter of confidence, security and assuredness. In Unit 16 *The Great Exhibition* it was pointed out that the Religious Census undertaken in 1851 suggested that religious practice was much less popular and central to the lives of the British people than, for example, Prince Albert assumed in his speech at the opening of the Exhibition. Similarly, in Units 1–3 *Introduction to History* and again in Unit 17 Arthur Marwick has referred to a passage from Horace Mann's Report on the Religious Census of 1851, and also to a passage from *Hard Times*, which indicate that the working classes, in particular, were alienated from the religious life of the Victorian churches.

In this section we shall look at the variety of Victorian religious life by focusing on three areas of conflict or crisis in Victorian religion:

1   The conflict between the Anglican establishment and the Nonconformist churches, that is, principally the Methodists, Congregationalists, Baptists, Presbyterians and Unitarians.

2   The conflict between Evangelical Protestantism and Catholicism.

3   The challenges posed to Victorian religion by the relationship between class and religion and by the rise of intellectual and moral criticisms of traditional Christian belief.

The argument underlying the whole discussion is that religion in Victorian Britain was not one thing but many, and the intensity with which the Victorians debated, argued and worried about religion was a reflection of the depth, and often the bitterness, of the divisions between Victorian religious believers.

That said, we must also continue to bear in mind that there remains one sense in which the religion of Victorian Britain was unified. As Geoffrey Best argues, in the section on 'Religion and the Social Order' in *Mid-Victorian Britain 1851–75*, to ask what made a person religious in the mid-Victorian context is to ask what made a person Christian. From a Christian standpoint, the period you are studying did see the emergence and steady growth of a wide range of unorthodox or heterodox religious groups. These included, for example, organized secularist groups which sought to 'convert' the working classes, especially, to political radicalism. There were also flourishing and important Jewish communities with an active religious tradition of their own. The fact remains, however, that, for the overwhelming majority, religion in 1850 meant Christianity. But if the kind of religious pluralism with which we are now so familiar did not exist, another kind of religious pluralism certainly did.

2.1 ANGLICANISM AND NONCONFORMITY

 Exercise

Please read extract II.1 in the Course Reader 'Edward Miall, from *The British Churches in Relation to the British People*, 1849'. Bearing in mind the information that Miall himself was a Nonconformist, Congregationalist minister, briefly write down the principal complaints Miall makes against Anglicanism, or, as he calls it, the 'civil establishment of Christianity'.

Discussion

Miall argues that the Church of England represents 'political religionism' because of the way in which the state interferes with its organization. Such 'civil establishments of Christianity' lack the characteristic of God's church: they are constructed and ordered by the 'powers that be' – that is, the secular powers.

Of the Anglican clergy, Miall says that three-quarters of them are ignorant of the gospel and are allied by their office to the aristocracy. They lack theological training and become clergy because of the worldly gains the Church of England offers. The worship they conduct is all formality and is also prone to 'priestism'. They also, especially in rural areas, oppose and prevent Nonconformity from preaching to the poor, even making it impossible for rooms to be hired by Nonconformists in some villages.

The bitterness of Miall's criticism is a reflection of the legal privileges which the Church of England possessed in the mid-nineteenth century, and the parallel legal and civil disabilities and inequalities suffered by Nonconformists. The 1851 Religious Census was to reveal not only that a large percentage of the population did not attend church at all on Census Sunday, but also, that of those who did attend, almost as many went to Nonconformist churches and chapels as to Anglican churches. The Census thus underlined the fact that – as Nonconformists had long argued – whatever special status was claimed for the established church, it was, by 1850, just one denomination among others, albeit still the largest single denomination and one officially protected by a mass of political and economic privileges which sustained its own status and discriminated against non-Anglicans.

This battery of privileges, or from a Nonconformist perspective, disabilities, had already been the focus of a series of religious-political confrontations in the quarter century before 1850. Between 1828 and 1850 a number of disabilities affecting both Nonconformists and Roman Catholics had already been repealed. There remained on the statute book, however, much other legislation which continued to discriminate against Nonconformists. Particular grievances were the exclusion of Nonconformists from taking degrees at Oxford and Cambridge Universities, the need to pay church rates for the upkeep of the established church, and the prevention of Nonconformists from being buried in Anglican churchyards. Behind such specific grievances, however, there stood the whole concept of an established church and its implied – and often actual – exclusion of Nonconformists from the mainstream of national life.

Faced with these disabilities, Victorian Nonconformity became increasingly militant in seeking reforms to remove the disadvantages. Edward Miall himself, for example, resigned from the Congregational ministry in 1844, after one of his congregation had been imprisoned for refusing to pay church rates, and founded the Society for the Liberation of Religion from State Patronage and Control, known popularly as the Liberation Society. As president of the Liberation Society, and as editor of the periodical *The Nonconformist*, Miall in many respects embodied the spirit of militant Nonconformity and its exploitation of Victorian pressure group politics in the attempt to secure the disestablishment of the Church

Units 18–19 Religion: Conformity and Controversy

of England. In the end Miall, and Victorian Nonconformity as a whole, were unable to achieve disestablishment as such, but in a series of piecemeal reforms, often wrung out of a grudging parliament after repeated failures, they did secure what has been called a 'gradual disestablishment' and a vastly increased degree of religious equality.

The political battles over these reforms, at both local and national level, and also over the question of educational reform and state provision of education (whether religious education should be included, and if so, what form it should take) meant that religion and politics, and especially the division between Anglican church and Nonconformist chapel, were inextricably bound up in Victorian society. It has, indeed, been argued that religion took so political a shape, and politics so religious a shape, in Victorian Britain that for many people it was impossible to separate the two. That may well be to overstate the case to the neglect of other equally important factors in political life, but it is certainly true that the development of Victorian party politics was affected by the religious issue. For example, in the emergence of the Liberal Party from a variety of interest and pressure groups, the role of Nonconformity was at least one important influence among others. Equally, the Victorian Conservative Party could rely upon a solid Anglican loyalty, despite exceptions to this pattern.

But it is important not to overstate such divisions. Thus the Parliamentary Liberal Party continued to be notably Anglican in composition even though Nonconformity provided one of its formative elements. The party was led, for much of the period in view here, by William Gladstone, who was a staunch Anglican High Churchman. Similarly, some sections of Victorian Nonconformity – Wesleyan Methodism for example – remained temperamentally conservative, and even supported the idea of religious establishment itself, whilst opposing those religious disabilities which they considered peripheral to the principle of Establishment.

When we add the complicating factor of the rise of the Labour movement, in both its trade-union and parliamentary forms, the relationship of religion and politics becomes even more complex. There is often a good deal of exaggeration in such statements as 'the British labour movement owes more to Methodism than to Marx', but an examination of early trade-union and Labour Party history reveals a high number of Nonconformists, and especially Methodists, involved in the emergent Labour movement. The example of the role of Primitive Methodism in the Agricultural Workers Union and the Durham Miners Union is one of the more striking cases. Primitive Methodism was in general much more working class than the older, Wesleyan Methodist tradition. Nor was it only Nonconformity that developed links with the late Victorian Labour movement. A significant minority of Anglican clergymen, especially Anglo-Catholic clergy working in inner-city slum parishes in the 1870s and 1880s, formed societies such as the Guild of St Matthew and the Christian Social Union whose aim was the development of a specifically Christian Socialism. In television programme 20 *Religion and Society in Victorian Bristol*, you will see something of the way in which one particular Anglican priest, Thomas Harvey, combined Christian Socialism and Anglo-Catholicism in a working-class suburb of Bristol.

2.2 EVANGELICALISM AND CATHOLICISM

The contrast between established religion and Nonconformity was one dimension of the variety and controversy inherent in Victorian religion. The tension between Evangelical Protestantism and Catholicism was another.

 Exercise

Please read extract II.2 in the Course Reader 'Letter from Lord John Russell to the Bishop of Durham'. What are the main points which the writer makes concerning Catholicism and Protestantism?

Discussion

Lord John Russell complains that recent measures taken by the Pope and the Roman Catholic authorities are 'insolent and insidious' and amount to 'aggression' against 'our Protestantism'. They imply a claimed supremacy which is inconsistent with the rights of the monarchy and the established church and which threatens the nation's spiritual independence. He also believes, however, that the 'liberty of Protestantism' has been enjoyed for too long in England for these Catholic claims to represent a real threat.

On the other hand, Lord John Russell is alarmed by the presence within the Church of England of clergy who introduce and advocate a variety of Catholic practices which he lists: the honouring of saints, claims of infallibility of the church, the sign of the cross, the recommendation of confession, penance and absolution.

This letter from Lord John Russell, then Prime Minister, was part of a public furore over the way in which the Roman Catholic church had, in 1850, restored its hierarchy of bishops to England – the restoration of an ecclesiastical administration which had not existed in England since the Reformation. What caused the furore was not the fact that the Roman Catholic bishops and dioceses were re-introduced but, rather, the tone of the accompanying announcements. Cardinal Wiseman, for example, the new Archbishop of Westminster, spoke of 'restoring Catholic England to its orbit in the ecclesiastical firmament'. This produced public outrage, press campaigns on the theme of 'no popery' and popular anti-Catholic riots. *Punch* carried anti-Catholic cartoons – see Figure 2. In 1851, parliament passed an Ecclesiastical Titles Bill which forbade the Roman Catholic church to use the diocesan titles which it had just re-established.

THE CHICHESTER EXTINGUISHER.

Bishop of Chichester. "GO! GO! YOU INSOLENT, REBELLIOUS BOY. – WHAT, WITH YOUR NONSENSE AND INCENSE AND CANDLES YOU'LL BE SETTING THE CHURCH ON FIRE."
Master P-ch-s. "JUST WHAT I'D LIKE TO DO. THERE!"

Figure 1 Bishop Gilbert of Chichester brandishes the 39 Articles against the Revd. John Purchas, Vicar of St James', Brighton, for using incense and altar candles. Purchas was subsequently prosecuted and the Privy Council found against him on 33 points of liturgical and ritual practice. (Source: Punch, October 1868)

In fact, however, the immediate Protestant-Catholic tension and conflict expressed in Lord John Russell's letter reflects a much deeper and more pervasive conflict in Victorian religious and cultural life. To examine this adequately we must briefly look at some developments before 1850.

In the century before the 1830s, not only the religious life of Britain but also its social and moral life had been radically changed by the impact of Evangelicalism. Both Methodism and Anglican Evangelicalism had, in the course of the mid- and late eighteenth century and the early nineteenth century, set their stamp upon the religion, morality and social ethos which the Victorians inherited.

But what was Evangelicalism? To that question there is no easy answer and what follows is a characterization rather than a definition. In specifically religious terms Evangelicalism involved a belief in the supreme authority of scripture, and a correspondingly negative view of good works, sacraments and the claims to authority of church or priesthood. It centred upon the experience of conversion, the vital religion of the heart, in which the individual experienced, first, a crushing sense of personal sin, and then the release of personal salvation, achieved by faith

LORD JACK THE GIANT KILLER.

Figure 2 Lord John Russell, the prime minister, prepares to wield the sword of the Ecclesiastical Titles Act against Cardinal Wiseman, while John Bull lends support and Mr Punch applauds. (Source: Punch, *Vol. 20, 1851)*

alone in the atoning sacrificial death of Christ. Mankind, in this theological tradition, was above all sinful, depraved, and in urgent and desperate need of salvation.

As a theological and religious ethos, Evangelicalism was not limited to any single denomination or set of denominations. It influenced the Anglican and Protestant Nonconformist churches in varying degrees and in a diffuse and widespread rather than highly specific manner. Moreover, it also manifested itself socially and culturally in a far-reaching range of values, standards and attitudes.

The impact of Evangelicalism on the Victorians and their culture has been described as 'the call to seriousness'. The Evangelical sense of the fallenness of man and the urgency of the need for salvation translated itself, in the moral and social sphere, into a passionate concern for moral improvement, the reformation of personal and social morality, and the intense desire to lead useful lives. For although Evangelicalism placed no value on good works as a means of salvation, it did insist on faith being expressed in morally upright lives. Duty, hard work, sobriety and earnestness became central elements in the Evangelical way of life. Among the practical consequences of this orientation was a concern for social reform – but through individual initiative, philanthropy, and the work of charitable societies, not through the attempt to change the fundamental social structure. This resulted in an intense emphasis upon the regulation of personal morality expressed through, for example, Sabbatarianism, temperance campaigns, attacks upon gambling and a particular concern over sexual morality. It also led to an intense stress upon the centrality of home and family as the focus and source of a secure moral foundation for both individual and society.

By the mid-nineteenth century, the significance of Evangelicalism was not so much its role as an organized and clearly identifiable movement but, rather, its legacy of attitudes and values which affected Victorian society even when Evangelicalism as a specific creed was rejected. Thus, for example, the intense seriousness, earnestness and sense of duty which runs through the life and work of prominent Victorians such as George Eliot or John Ruskin are, in part at least, a tribute to Evangelical upbringings and to the diffused cultural legacy of Evangelicalism – despite their open and radical disavowal of Evangelicalism as a specific creed. Radio programme 10 *George Eliot: The Search for Secular Answers* focuses on this theme.

As far as Evangelicalism in its more narrowly religious sense is concerned, by 1850, and increasingly during the period we are studying here, it became a more defensive, more inward looking and narrowly combative force in Victorian religious life. In particular, Evangelicalism became aggressively opposed to what it understood to be the threats of rationalism, Romanism and ritualism. The first of these we will consider in a later section of these units. The latter two, Romanism and ritualism, are more immediately relevant.

The intense anti-Catholicism which you have encountered in the letter from Lord John Russell, and also to some extent in Edward Miall's references to 'priestism', had complicated origins. Victorian anti-Catholicism was not simply a religious issue. It was also bound up with a popular, urban working-class patriotism which crudely identified Roman Catholicism or 'Romanism' with foreign political influence and also with a popular anti-Irish, anti-immigrant prejudice. Urban anti-Catholic feeling was often as much, or more, anti-Irish, or anti-immigrant as anti-Catholic. That said, the specifically religious element in Victorian anti-Catholicism was still an important aspect of the Victorian religious world.

The Evangelical revival had reinforced the Protestantism of British life and, in the early decades of the nineteenth century, appeared to be the dominant religious style. In the 1830s and 1840s however, there occurred a remarkable resurgence of the Catholic spirit and tradition *within* the Anglican communion, as well as a revival in the English Roman Catholic community. The precise origins and motivations of the Oxford Movement, as the revival in Anglicanism came to be known, lie outside the boundaries of this case study. What is important here is the fact that, initially under the leadership of a group of Oxford dons, especially John Keble, Edward Pusey and John Henry Newman, a significant section of the Church of England rediscovered and re-emphasized the Catholic tradition *within* Anglicanism. Alongside the Bible they stressed the role of liturgy, sacraments, hierarchy, priesthood and the authority of the church and its tradition. They also cultivated an interest in history, especially the mediaeval period, and in so doing both reflected and contributed to a characteristically Victorian flight into the past as one response to the challenges of industrialization and its consequent social upheaval.

The supporters of the Oxford Movement were also known as Tractarians because, during the early years of the movement, they presented their arguments in a series of 'Tracts for the Times'. Some members of the Oxford Movement were particularly concerned to promote the building and restoration of churches in what they considered to be the correct 'catholic' style. To further their aims, they formed, in 1839, the Ecclesiological Society.

The contrasting and often conflicting emphases of Evangelicalism and Catholicism – especially the Anglo-Catholic tradition within Anglicanism – were reflected in theology, in worship and in the style, shape and design of the churches and chapels in which Victorian Evangelicals and Catholics worshipped. Television programmes 18 and 19 on Anglican and Nonconformist church building are important here. Whilst concentrating on the architecture of a number of Anglican and Nonconformist churches and chapels, these programmes also reveal a great deal about the ways in which the Catholic and Evangelical traditions varied in their worship, theology and social backgrounds. The programmes also show how varied Victorian Anglicanism and Nonconformity were within themselves. When you read the Broadcast Notes for these programmes, you will find that they ask a number of questions about these contrasts between different theological traditions and denominations. It will help your viewing of these programmes and your answers to the questions in the Broadcast Notes if you make some preliminary notes on the differences between various theological groups and denominations that emerge in the discussion here (roughly, pp.10–15).

For Evangelicals, the resurgence of Catholic tradition, belief and practice represented a challenge and threat. From a position of confidence and dominance, Evangelicalism became more defensive and combative, fearing that the Oxford Movement would undermine the Protestant nature of British life from within, a fear which was fostered by a number of conversions to Roman Catholicism by leading members of the Oxford Movement – John Henry Newman's conversion in 1845 being merely the most notable. It was in this context that the announcement by the Pope of the restoration of a hierarchy of Catholic bishops caused such a furore in 1850.

The popular agitation which followed involved attacks upon both Roman Catholicism and upon the Anglo-Catholic tradition within the Church of England which, as the last paragraphs of Lord John Russell's letter indicate, was continuing the work begun by the Oxford Movement in the 1830s and early 1840s. The ironic aspect of the popular outcry against Roman Catholicism in 1850–51 was that, in the longer perspective of the forty-year period that we are studying, the Roman Catholic community in Britain continued to experience an impressive revival, while popular anti-Catholic feeling for the most part became directed more against *Anglo*-Catholicism than against *Roman* Catholicism. Indeed, by 1889 Cardinal Manning, successor to the bitterly resented Wiseman, had become a respected public figure, a temperance advocate, and an admired supporter of the poor and the agricultural and dock workers. English Roman Catholicism, aided by both Irish immigration and the conversion of a significant number of highly able Anglicans, became a flourishing religious subculture during the mid- and late Victorian period. Anglo-Catholicism also achieved the status of a flourishing subculture within Victorian Anglicanism, but it did so only at the cost of a long and very bitter struggle. In 1874 a Public Worship Regulation Act sought to prohibit within the Church of England the kinds of 'catholic' ritual and liturgical practices referred to by Lord John Russell. Again, as you can see in Figure 3, a cartoon from *Punch*, the issue provoked popular comment and controversy. The result was a series of prosecutions, convictions and the imprisonment of 'Ritualist' Anglican clergy. Only in the decade-and-a-half after 1890 was a workable compromise reached within Anglicanism — a compromise which effectively left the Ritualists free to worship as they wished, at least for the most part. Television programme 18, which contrasts All Saints, Margaret Street, with St Marks, Dalston, reflects these 'ritualist' controversies.

I hope this discussion of some of the varieties of religion in Victorian Britain, together with television programmes 18, 19 and 20, has demonstrated that the religious life of the Victorians was not only intense but also complex and many-sided. To recapitulate briefly: I have argued that a series of tensions or diversities lies at the heart of Victorian religion. Anglicanism and establishment over/against Nonconformity; Protestantism, Anglican and Nonconformist over/against Roman and Anglo–Catholicism; Anglicanism itself divided between High and Low Church, Catholic and Evangelical – and, as you will see in the next section, further complicated by a Broad Church or 'Liberal' party. Before leaving the question of the range of Christian denominations in Victorian Britain, however, we must look at the variety within Nonconformity.

Victorian Nonconformity was a much maligned phenomenon. Perhaps the classic attack upon it was that of Matthew Arnold in 1869 in *Culture and Anarchy*. According to Arnold, Nonconformity was merely narrow-minded, provincial and philistine:

> In the same way let us judge the religious organisations which we see all around us. Do not let us deny the good and the happiness which they have accomplished; but do not

"BLACK SHEEP."

Figure 3 Archbishop of Canterbury Archibald Campbell Tait attempts to keep ritualist sheep in order by means of the Public Worship Regulation Bill. Some of the ritualist sheep choose to leap the wall and go to the Roman Catholic Church. The bill became law but failed to suppress ritualism. (Source: Punch, *March 1874)*

let us fail to see clearly that their idea of human perfection is narrow and inadequate, and that the Dissidence of Dissent and the Protestantism of the Protestant religion will never bring humanity to its true goal. As I said with regard to wealth: Let us look at the life of those who live in and for it, – so I say with regard to the religious organisations. Look at the life imaged in such a newspaper as the *Nonconformist*, – a life of jealousy of the Establishment, disputes, tea-meetings, openings of chapels, sermons; and then think of it as an ideal of a human life completing itself on all sides, and aspiring with all its organs after sweetness, light, and perfection! (Arnold, *Culture and Anarchy*)

In contrast to Arnold's usually liberal, broad-minded outlook, this comment is a peculiarly English, Anglican and establishment remark. In fact, mid- and late Victorian Nonconformity was a rich and varied world. On the one hand there were the highly cultivated middle- and upper-class chapels of the major provincial cities in whose civic life Nonconformity played a major role, as for example, in the Congregational contribution to the life of Birmingham (of which you will hear in more detail in radio programme 15 *R. W. Dale and the Civic Gospel*), the Wesleyan Methodist contribution to Leeds, or the Unitarian contribution to the politics and cultural life of Liverpool. By 1890, urban Nonconformity had also developed the phenomenon of the Institutional Church, the attempt to provide an entire religious, social, cultural, educational and recreational world for the church member and for the converts they hoped to win from the working-class communities in which such churches were situated.

Geoffrey Best gives details, on pages 217–18 of *Mid-Victorian Britain 1851–75*, of the sheer range of religious, social and cultural activities which Nonconformist chapels often provided. Quite rightly he also points out that much of this activity was clearly recreational; quite as much as it was religious. Negatively, such churches can be dismissed as the despairing effort of Nonconformity to keep hold of its members, and especially its sons and daughters, in an age of increasing secular leisure and recreational opportunities. They can also be seen as an ambitious and remarkable attempt to broaden the interests and cultural integration of a Nonconformity increasingly free of civil disabilities and thus able to seek more positive roles in society. Television programme 19 on Nonconformity in Dukinfield, Newcastle-under-Lyme and Saltaire illustrates both the diversity and continuity within Nonconformity and, again, draws attention to the range of social, educational and recreational roles which a Nonconformist church or chapel might provide.

Alongside such sophisticated middle-class urban and suburban Nonconformity there also existed a Nonconformity of small chapel communities in rural areas and in small industrial, mining and fishing villages. The social significance of such communities is nowhere better illustrated than in the biographies of late Victorian trade-union and labour leaders who frequently testify to the deepening and broadening effect of a childhood and adolescence in a chapel environment. The contrast between such urban and rural Nonconformity was not, of course, total. The point to note is that Nonconformity could and did flourish in both urban and rural settings – it was not, as is often implied, simply strong in the towns and cities, and weak in the countryside.

Finally, beyond the world of the recognized Nonconformist traditions, the mid- and late Victorian period saw a proliferation of individual chapels, mission halls, gospel halls, temperance churches, railway missions, city missions and so forth. The sheer diversity and individuality of such institutions makes any very definite conclusions about them difficult, but it is clear that together they represented a considerable popular religious subculture, especially within the Victorian city. The concluding section of television programme 20 *Religion and Society in Victorian Bristol*, which looks at Hebron and Mount Zion chapels, takes us into just this milieu.

Nor does this exhaust the dimensions of Victorian religion. The religiousness of Victorian life was not only a matter of churches, chapels and mission halls, inter-denominational quarrels, and the politics of establishment and dissent. There was also the sheer volume of religious literature, both popular and more specialized.

In Memoriam, and especially the sentiments of those two lines on faith and doubt, has been called the representative poem of mid-nineteenth-century Britain, precisely because it expressed so sharply the sense of faith seeking assurance in the face of doubt and challenges to faith.

In the 1830s and 1840s a whole series of early Victorian intellectuals made the transition from faith, through doubt to some form of agnosticism or disbelief. George Eliot was one of the most notable examples, but she was far from alone. The causes of such crises of faith were complex but usually involved moral questioning of traditional Christian doctrines, such as the sacrificial and atoning death of Christ, the concept of hell and eternal punishment, or the morality of some Old Testament miracles. With this there was often mixed a growing critical awareness of the historical and uncertain nature of so much of the biblical narrative and the witness of geology to the age of the earth, with all that that implied for a literal interpretation of the first chapters of Genesis. Such doubts and questionings found expression in painting as well as in novels and poetry, and in the letters and autobiographical writings of Victorian intellectuals. Thus, when you read section 6 of these units on Victorian painters and religion, you will find that these themes appear again. The painting by William Dyce of *Pegwell Bay*, for example, has geology and its implications as one of its themes. Similarly, H. A. Bowler intended his painting *The Doubt: 'Can These Dry Bones Live?'* to be a meditation on Tennyson's *In Memoriam* and the latter's painful, ambiguous struggle with the theme of mortality and the credibility – or incredibility – of hopes of immortality. (For a reproduction of *The Doubt*, see Plate 38 in the *Illustration Booklet*.)

For a significant number of mid-Victorian intellectuals therefore, the crisis of faith was a painful and personal reality some two decades or more before Darwin and the theory of evolution, and it is this strand of Victorian experience that *In Memoriam* represents.

But if the Victorian crisis of faith was already a reality in 1850, it is also true that in the decades after 1850 that crisis both deepened and broadened as traditional Christian belief was confronted by challenges from liberal thought within the church, from the continuing developments in scientific discovery and thought, and from philosophical thought. Thus, in sections 4 and 5 of these units, we shall focus on just these issues.

Before that, however, we shall first consider a particular example of the *variety* and *vitality* of Victorian religious life, namely the role of music in Victorian religious worship and, in particular, the popularity and significance of hymns and hymn-singing.

3 MUSIC IN VICTORIAN WORSHIP

3.1 HISTORICAL BACKGROUND

If we were to ask you what the most typical musical element in Christian worship is today, you would probably reply, 'hymns'. Most services, of whatever denomination, include several; often they are the only music. Moreover, many of them have achieved widespread familiarity outside the context of worship: 'Onward Christian Soldiers' and 'Abide with Me', 'There is a Green Hill' and 'All Things Bright and Beautiful', are deeply buried in the cultural foundations of British life. But the ubiquity of hymn singing is relatively recent; to a considerable extent it is the product of developments in the Victorian period. At the beginning of the nineteenth century probably only a minority of worshippers regularly sang or heard a hymn. For many Nonconformists, hymns had long been important; they offered the opportunity to express personal religious emotion and experience: guilt, salvation, grace, God's love, etc. But the Church of England (and the established Church of Scotland) traditionally mistrusted hymns. Only the psalms were authorized, sung to a small number of tunes, many dating from the sixteenth and seventeenth centuries; this was because psalms were scriptural, hence divine, whereas hymns were human products unsuitable for inclusion in acts of worship. Some Nonconformists — particularly in Scotland — held similar views. Evangelicals sang hymns, and their influence was growing; otherwise, hymns were rare in Anglican services. But the strength of the Nonconformist denominations was increasing. And in 1820 hymns were in effect legalized for Anglicans. After that, their popularity grew quickly. The Oxford Movement believed hymns were legitimate (because the early and medieval church had sung them), and under its influence the 'high' wing of the church swung in favour. By the 1850s large numbers of hymn collections were being published, and in 1861 *Hymns Ancient and Modern* appeared — a collection which, although Anglican, in time became one of the first truly 'national' hymn books. The period up to *c.* 1880 then saw a boom, which affected all denominations, in the publication of hymnals and the production of new hymns. The universality of the hymn, its position as an epitome of Victorian religion, was established.

Not all hymn tunes were published in 'standard' notation. An important development in the Victorian period was the growth of the so-called 'sight-singing' movement using 'sol-fa' systems. There were several musical educators who devised and promoted systems, alternatives to the traditional staff notation, that aimed to make musical literacy simpler and thus more accessible to the mass of people. The most successful and enduring version of these systems was devised by the Congregationalist minister, John Curwen (1816–80). In 1841 Curwen was asked by the Congregationalist church to investigate ways of teaching singing at Sunday schools. Curwen was not a musician, but he was a talented teacher. He taught himself to read music by adapting a system invented by an East Anglian schoolmistress, Sarah Glover. Curwen's version of the tonic sol-fa method became widely used for secular as well as for church music of many denominations.

The principal feature of the system is that each note of the major (or minor) scale is given a name that does not change, irrespective of the key that a given piece of music is in. So the first (or home, or tonic) note of the scale is always called *doh*, the second *ray*, the third *me*, and so on (*fah, soh, lah, te, doh*). An equally simple system was drawn up for rhythmic notation, but it has to be said the system worked, and still works best, when used for fairly simple melodic lines, and fairly straightforward rhythmic phrases — such as those used in hymns.

The sight-singing movement was important to Victorian musical education generally: potentially it enabled people from all classes to participate in the sort of music-making which depends on being able to read a score, and to some extent it thus encouraged them to sing the same kinds of music. The movement was particularly important for congregational singing because it provided a new way by which four-part singing, that is two female parts (soprano and alto) and two male parts (tenor and bass), could be promoted. This caused a growth of interest and enjoyment in congregational singing.

In an age of fierce doctrinal and inter-denominational wrangling, the singing of hymns — even sometimes the *same* hymns — was a practice which provided some common ground. Moreover, a considerable level of agreement was reached on the general role of music in church, and this measure of agreement could be regarded as an aspect of a wider consensus in mid-Victorian society. At the beginning of the century, there was a wide variety of opinions on what kind of music (if any) was appropriate, and how it should be performed and by whom. The cathedrals maintained an élite tradition of complex composed music for choir and organ, most parts of the services being set to music. Some parish churches, usually 'high' in outlook, tried to ape this practice. Most, however, heard only sung or chanted psalms and perhaps responses, performed by a volunteer choir or just priest and parish clerk. Evangelicals favoured congregational hymns and were happy to use tunes from secular sources — theatrical, sentimental or graceful pieces in contemporary styles. Much the same was true of Methodists, and a typically 'Methodist' tune appeared, which was quite elaborate in texture and structure, with considerable repetition of words and contrasts between men's and women's voices, but tuneful and easy to sing. More radical Nonconformists usually insisted on more austere tunes of an older type, while 'low' church Anglicans — concerned above all for order, decorum and 'rationality' in their worship — often advocated services led by an organ and a choir of 'charity children' performing pieces modelled on contemporary art music. In village churches a tradition of 'country psalmody' had grown up, in which amateur choirs and bands rendered quite complex psalm settings and anthems composed for them by local musicians, often unschooled, in a style which was enough of a vernacular, 'vulgar' variant of earlier art music practices to attract the general opposition of urban, middle-class opinion. Other 'popular' practices included the first 'folk hymns' of American origin, associated with the religious revival of 1807, which gave birth to Primitive Methodism, and remnants of the so-called 'old way' of psalm singing, in which unaccompanied congregations sang the original Reformation tunes very slowly in a style full of elaborate ornament (this approach still survives in some of the Western Isles of Scotland). In the eighteenth century, conflict between proponents of 'reform' and 'improvement' on the one hand, and those of entrenched traditions, congregational rights and popular 'folk' practices on the other was endemic.

It would not be true to say that all these distinctions and conflicts had disappeared by the late Victorian period. At one extreme, radical Evangelicals and Nonconformists maintained their approach, while 'gospel song' of the type associated with the Salvation Army appeared; at the other end, some Anglo-Catholics restricted themselves to unaccompanied plainsong, the music of the medieval church. However, in between, there was a broad acceptance of a rather eclectic repertory which included some quite complex music, but which was centred on the 'Victorian hymn'. Similarly, an acceptance of professional musical arrangements was balanced by stress on congregational participation. This drew on an eclectic range of styles but all were regarded as 'respectable'. Earlier popular traditions had largely been destroyed. The consensus embraced almost the whole Church of England and the more mainstream and middle-class Nonconformists, whose hymn books now included many of the same hymns as those of the Anglicans, even if their congregations (probably trained in the sight-singing movement) often played a larger role, their choirs a lesser one. One might argue that this consensus represents a final victory for 'reform' over tradition, authority over local discretion, the 'artistic' over the 'popular', professional standards over congregational autonomy, after disputes lasting for generations. Yet, despite being largely organized 'from above' by clergy, scholars, professional musicians and social élites, the new consensus became popular; or at least, the considerable extent to which it *was* accepted can be seen as one facet of the cultural consensus which developed within Victorian society, beyond its conflicts and disputes (this argument is made in N. Temperley, *The Music of the English Parish Church*).

3.2 'HYMNS ANCIENT AND MODERN'

The idea of a comprehensive hymn book was relatively new. Before *Hymns Ancient and Modern* almost all collections were partial and local: often they represented just the repertory of a particular church. The project was initiated by a high church group, and the first edition, under the influence of the Oxford Movement, included many translations of Latin hymns. But subsequent editions added more recent types and many new hymns and by the 'Standard' edition of 1875 the book was a synthesis capable of acting as a truly national collection, throughout the Church of England at least. Its success was astonishing. By 1894, it was used, for example, in three out of five London churches, and in rural areas its dominance was almost total. Its cultural influence has also been extraordinary. Many still familiar hymns were introduced in *Hymns Ancient and Modern* and many still current associations between a particular hymn and a particular tune were first made there. Indeed, during the First World War it was noted by one observer that soldiers would turn easily to *Hymns Ancient and Modern* because it was 'a genuine part of our folklore' (First World War officer quoted in A. Wilkinson, *The Church of England and the First World War*, p. 158). And even today many of those hymns are part of most English people's mental furniture. In part at least, this is probably because of the book's success in symbolizing and assisting in the re-shaping of the Church of England as a broad national church after the disputes of the mid-Victorian period.

For all the variety of hymn tunes, sources and tune styles in *Hymns Ancient and Modern*, it did establish a new and particular type, the 'Victorian' hymn. The richly coloured, emotional, perhaps sentimental, but always accessible tunes – many by the editor W. H. Monk, many others by J. B. Dykes – could be put to  texts of almost any persuasion: this consensus was a cultural, not a doctrinal one.

Exercise

Look, for example at the text of 'The King of Love' (*Cassette Notes 1*, p. 41). While the writer's stress on his personal relationshp with the Shepherd-Saviour may perhaps be attributed to the general influence of evangelicalism in the nineteenth century, there is nothing otherwise to link these words with any particular doctrinal tendency. The music, however, is a classic example of the new *Hymns Ancient and Modern*. Listen to the recording (Cassette 5, side 1, band 2a) and then read the following discussion.

Discussion

The harmonies are rich, with lots of chord changes and an up-to-date style. Notice the skilful writing for the lower voices; if you listen hard to alto, tenor and bass, you will hear that they have quite a lot of interesting melodic movement of their own: without all four parts, a performance would be much less satisfying. This then is a miniature work of art; it acknowledges the desire of middle-class congregations for a 'professional' product and their acceptance of the choir's leading role. At the same time, the tune is simple, even banal; it moves almost entirely in steps and is easy for the layperson to sing. The congregation is invited to participate; it is flattered, 'turned . . . into a section of the church "orchestra" '

(Temperley, p. 306). The similarity of the style to that of the contemporary secular part-song is significant, for that genre too combined accessibility, expressive harmony and a flatteringly up-to-date musical idiom, in a mixture suitable for the middle-class drawing room.

3.3 THE OXFORD MOVEMENT

As we said, the ideas of the Oxford Movement were of considerable influence on the contents of early editions of *Hymns Ancient and Modern*. But originally the Tractarians' tastes in liturgical music focused above all on the unaccompanied chant (plainsong) of the medieval church. This is not surprising, in the light of their wide antiquarian interests and their enthusiasm for the Middle Ages, for gothic church architecture and for ceremonial. Plainsong could represent continuity with the pre-Reformation church. It was archaic and therefore suited the idea that the church should be set apart from secular life, that religion should be mysterious and other-worldly. In style it was felt to be austere, objective and impersonal, therefore more suited to liturgical needs than the subjective, emotional style of Protestant hymns. Lastly, being unaccompanied and melodically simple, it was thought to be ideally suited to collective performance, which was the Tractarians' ideal, as it was of the early Church.

There was much research, several important publications and considerable experiment in sympathetic churches. But the use of plainsong never exceeded twenty per cent of London churches (less elsewhere), and after 1875 even this declined. More important, perhaps, was the fact that many plainsong melodies were 'adapted', 'modernized' and given a harmonic accompaniment, appearing in this form in 'general' hymn books such as *Hymns Ancient and Modern*.

The hymn 'Aeterna Christi Munera', which you have already heard in its medieval form (Cassette 3, side 1, band 4), was one of many to be translated and its tune adapted for modern usage. On Cassette 5 (Side 1, band 2c) you can hear a verse sung in the version included in the first edition of *Hymns Ancient and Modern*, followed by a verse sung in the version from the 1875 edition.

Exercise

Listen to all three versions, then briefly describe the main musical differences between (1) the medieval version (a) and the 1861 version (b); (2) the 1861 version and the 1875 version (c). Remember the elements discussed in the *Introduction to Music* units — particularly rhythm and texture. Only one or two points are needed for each comparison.

Discussion

1 Version (a) is unaccompanied, whereas in (b) the tune is given a harmonic setting sung in four parts. In (a) there is only one note-length, with a pause on the last note of each phrase. There is no regular pattern of accents; instead the accentuation follows that of the words: the music is not *metrical*. The effect is very fluid. In (b) there is still no regular pattern of accents, no metre; but there is greater variety of note-length (especially at the ends of phrases). The effect is that the tune sounds rhythmically more constrained, more 'structured'.

2 In (c) the note-lengths are changed further. Now they are so arranged that strong accents fit into a regular pattern; the tune has been put into a metre, three in a bar:

```
For they the Church----'s prin------ces are,-----Tri--um--phant lea--ders in the
    and|  1    and    2    3 and| 1  2  3 and| 1    2   and  3    and  | 1  2  and 3 and|
war,---------- In heaven-ly courts a warr-ior band, ------------------ True
  1    2    3  and| 1    and    2  and  3 and|  1    2    3 | 1   2    3      and|
lights to light-----en e--------very land.------------
    1   and  2    3  and| 1  2    3  and| 1     2       3|
```

Through the three versions, there is an overall trend away from fluidity, towards pattern and regularity. Medieval melody has been, perhaps, brought down to earth, in a process which one might see as analogous to the relationship between Pre-Raphaelite artists and medieval painting.

3.4 THE CHORAL REVIVAL

In a sense, the Tractarians' insistence on ritual was diverted from its purest focus and fused with pre-existing tendencies, particularly among the high wing of the Anglican church, to promote a more artistically serious, ceremonially splendid kind of worship. The result was the 'Choral revival'. The role model was Leeds parish church where, in the 1840s, the notable composer S. S. Wesley, who was organist there, turned it virtually into a cathedral. Choirs began wearing the white, quasi-clerical garments known as surplices. Organs were promoted (for, as one advocate said in 1820, 'an instrument powerful enough to drown the voices of parish clerk, charity children, and congregation, is an inestimable blessing'). Services were either chanted (usually to modern harmonized chants, not plainsong) or sung in composed settings. Elaborate anthems were enjoyed, sometimes from the cathedral repertory, but often newly composed: a torrent of choral music in cheap editions poured out to meet the needs of the new market. A desire for decorum coupled with a belief in 'improvement' resulted in a 'superior' kind of service which became commonplace in parish churches and also many of the larger Nonconformist chapels in the 1860s and '70s. Large sums were spent on 'beautifying' worship in this way. The service of the eucharist which you will see in Television programme 18 *The Victorian High Church*, represents the continued development of this trend. However, you should realize that the mixed adult choir is a twentieth-century development within Anglicanism. In the nineteenth century, the treble part would have been sung by boys only, who were educated in the choir school attached to the church.

One of the most popular cathedral services (still widely used today) was the *Evening Service in D minor* (1855) by the Cambridge organist, choir master and composer (and Professor of Music at the age of twenty-two!) T. A. Walmisley (1814–56). The Magnificat from this service can be heard on Cassette 5, side 1, band 2e. Unlike hymns, pieces of this kind are 'through-composed', that is, the composer matched changing words with ever-changing music rather than repeating the same music over and over. Obviously, it demands an expert choir and a good organ, and the congregation is meant to listen in a spirit of contemplation, part aesthetic, part spiritual. You will notice a rich harmonic vocabulary, sophisticated use of the organ, in an independent as well as an accompanying role, and a wide variety of dynamics, expressive effects and textures, with contrasts between chordal and unison singing, boys' voices and men's, close and wide spacing, and so on; also, just before the end ('As it was in the beginning, world without end') there is some impressive counterpoint. Listen to it before you proceed.

3.5 'POPULAR' CHOIRS AND BANDS

A negative aspect of Victorian 'improvement' in church music was the campaign to abolish 'country psalmody'. Reforming clergy and 'cultivated' musicians advocated 'proper' choirs singing approved music in a decorous manner and encouraged the installing of organs (or, failing them, barrel organs) to replace the small bands (usually combinations of fiddle, cello, bassoon, clarinet and flute). The 'popular' tradition was criticized both on account of the alleged vulgarity and incompetence of the music and performing techniques, and of the power the choirs and bands could exercise over the conduct of services (conflicts between vicar, musicians, congregations and even the local patron were common). The choirs had originated in the early eighteenth century while the accompanying bands flourished from c. 1770 to c. 1830. By the early nineteenth century their earlier repertory of psalm settings, hymns and anthems was being supplemented by music derived from urban Evangelical and Methodist sources; and indeed some performed in local chapel as well as parish church, even travelling round a circuit of venues. By c. 1850 most seem to have disbanded, but in the west country many continued up to the 1890s.

The novelist, **Thomas Hardy,** wrote sympathetically about the old village choirs and bands (notably in his novel *Under the Greenwood Tree*): his grandfather had led the band at Puddletown in Dorset (replaced by a barrel organ in 1845) and his father played in the band at nearby Stinsford. The Dorset repertory was very rich in carols and 'Rejoice This Glorious Day Is Come' (Cassette 5, side 1, band 2f) is found in manuscripts from both Puddletown and the Hardy family collection.

 Exercise

Listen to 'Rejoice This Glorious Day Is Come' and try to write down some ways in which its musical style differs from the music you have heard up to now in this section. Again think of the main musical elements — melody, rhythm, harmony, timbre and texture — and bear in mind musical structure as well.

 Discussion

Though, like most hymns, it is strophic (that is, all verses are sung to the same music), its structure is far more elaborate than that of the average hymn, with an instrumental introduction and interlude, contrasts of vocal texture, and a second section (repeated) which contains much word repetition and some simple imitative counterpoint (actually the counterpoint is more like antiphony: call and response between pairs of voices). Though the structure is quite elaborate, however, the style is very different from that of the Walmisley Magnificat. Rather, the strong, simple harmonies, the contrasts between simple counterpoint or antiphony and block chords, and the jaunty rhythms hark back to eighteenth-century music, notably to Handel, one of the main sources for 'Country Psalmody' style. If you listen hard, you might also notice that the harmonic writing sounds a bit odd at times: the spacings and sometimes the choice of notes are gauche by conventional 'textbook' criteria. Similarly, the word-setting is often 'incorrect' with weak syllables given strong musical accents.

There is no evidence, however, that the country people who performed this music (mostly artisans) thought of these characteristics as failings. While you will study Victorian popular culture more directly in later units (Units 22–26), it may be worth introducing here the suggestion that the same materials can be used differently but with equal validity by different social groups. And, though the tradition of 'Country Psalmody' was crushed by the strength of more 'respectable' Victorian taste, other equally popular religious musical practices, associated with mainly lower class groups, arose in the nineteenth century. We shall look at some of these in the next two sections.

3.6 EVANGELICALS AND NONCONFORMISTS

As we saw earlier, congregational singing was particularly important for Evangelicals and Nonconformists. The source of this popularity was the belief that faith should be expressed by individuals themselves, in music as in prayer, rather than being expressed *for* them by a choir or priest; but this often led to vibrant, skilled, and in some cases quite elaborate performing traditions which were valued for aesthetic and social as well as religious reasons. Such traditions were very strong in Wales.

There, the interest in hymn singing as an activity in its own right, beyond being simply a part of congregational worship, is exemplified with the advent of the festivals known as Gymanfa Ganu (Festival of (Hymn) Singing). They were founded by the Calvinistic Methodist minister and hymnist, John Roberts (1822–77); he was also known by the bardic name Ieuan Gwyllt. The Gymanfa Ganu were held to coincide with religious festivals, most particularly Easter and Whitsun. They included not just hymns but some of the most popular choruses from eighteenth- and nineteenth-century oratorio as well. These festivals became enormously important social as well as religious occasions and it is no accident that from this time Handel and Haydn became popular names for Welsh parents to choose for boys.

The tradition of Welsh hymn writing was well founded in the eighteenth century, most particularly by William Williams (Pantycelyn) (1717–91) and Ann Griffiths (1776–1805) who, though she died at the age of 29, is responsible for hymn-poems which are regarded by many as some of the finest literary achievements in the Welsh language. However, it was not until 1839 when John Roberts (1807–76) published *Caniadau y Cysegr* that there was a Welsh language hymn collection for the use of congregations. Many of these hymns were set to tunes of Welsh, usually folksong, origin.

3.7 GOSPEL SONG

The foundation of the Salvation Army in 1878 (it had existed as the East London Christian Mission since 1865) provided a new dimension to the use of hymns in the service of religion, but even here there are strong antecedents in the music of other religious movements of the nineteenth century.

Salvationism is a brand of revivalism and it has been described by the historian Victor Bailey in the following terms:

> Salvationism was identified by the emphasis upon a personal relationship with God; and by an intense congregational participation in the service. There was no intellectualism and little theology [. . . and] a complete faith in the atoning work of Christ, a faith which could lead to conversion, an instant flight from the terror of hell to the assurance of heaven. (Bailey, 'Salvation Army Riots . . .', pp. 235–6)

The most obvious outward manifestation of Salvationism is, of course, the military metaphor which pervades almost every aspect of its organization, presentation and vocabulary. Indeed, most Salvationists, particularly in the nineteenth century, and perhaps many today, would not acknowledge the existence of the metaphorical. They *were* the army; their weapons goodness, purity and the atoning power of God. Their adversaries sin, evil and the corrupting power of the devil. The devil's agents were plain to see in the beer houses of the cities, in the music halls, and in the poverty of the streets that surrounded them.

The enemy was not to be conquered by an intellectual address from a distant pulpit but by being tackled head-on in campaigns where his works were rife. It is important to emphasize the total conviction with which the early Salvationists addressed their task under the charismatic leadership of General William Booth. Accounts by Salvationists of early campaigns of the army talk of them marching 'in the ecstasy of their witness'. The Salvation Army also had to deal with considerable abuse, intimidation and physical attack from members of the general public. Much of this abuse emanated from those of various classes who opposed temperance. But also there were organized groups of urban youths – mainly labourers and semi-skilled workers – who, calling themselves the 'Skeleton Army', marshalled themselves into coherent ranks specifically to intimidate the Salvationists.

The hymns of the Salvationists had to be rousing, inspiring and capable of being heard in the open air. Most of them had these qualities, but also, like the

Army itself, they possessed an alchemy of the sacred and the secular, the spiritual and the vernacular.

It was never the intention of General Booth that the quality of the performance of Salvationist music or the intricacy of the writing should have any great prominence. The primary aim was that the music should make an impact on people by being immediate, striking, simple and memorable:

> Merely professional music is always a curse and should you ever find a choir in connection with any hall in this mission, I give you my authority to take a besom and sweep it out, promising that you do so as lovingly as possible.
>
> You must sing good tunes. Let it be a good tune to begin with. I don't care much whether you call it secular or sacred. I rather enjoy robbing the devil of his choice tunes, and, after his subjects themselves, music is about the best commodity he possesses. It is like taking the enemy's guns and turning them against him.
>
> However, come it whence it may, let us have a real tune, that is, a melody with some distinct air in it, that one can take hold of, which people can learn, nay which makes them learn it, which takes hold of them and goes on humming in the mind until they have mastered it. That is the sort of a tune to help you; it will preach to you, and bring you believers and converts. (Quoted in Boon, *Sing the Happy Song*, p. 5)

From the 1880s, Salvationists used brass and percussion instruments to accompany their singing. This practice originated in Salisbury where a builder called Charles Fry and three of his sons gave up their business to serve Salvationism as musicians. (One of the sons, Bert Fry, was an expert in the tonic sol-fa method.) In a short time, the practice of bands accompanying Salvationist hymns became common. The use of bands (these were quite different from the early nineteenth-century church bands) gave Salvationist music a distinctive flavour. But few of the early Salvationist hymns were entirely new.

There was already a substantial revivalist movement in Britain, whose worship was characterized by 'gospel hymns'. The main influence here was the American Evangelist duo of Dwight Lyman Moody (1837–99) and Ira David Sankey (1840–1908). Moody was a charismatic preacher who employed Sankey, a singer and organist, as musical director of his church in Chicago. They made their first British tour in 1872 and were enormously successful. Moody's preaching and Sankey's singing were a persuasive combination. These great revivalist meetings were the impetus for a number of gospel hymn book publications. The most widely circulated of these was *Sacred Songs and Solos* which in a number of editions contained well over a thousand pieces, including a large number of Sankey's own hymns. Moreover, the fact that the revivalism of Sankey and Moody was highly influential in Scotland and Ulster as well as in England meant that *Sacred Songs and Solos* became widely used among Evangelicals throughout Britain — indeed, it could be said to be one of the first truly 'national' collections of hymns, albeit in a very informal and unofficial way. (You will encounter the Salvation Army and the significance of hymns as a means of evangelizing the working classes again in A102, first in Television programme 20, *Religion and Society in Victorian Bristol*, and then in Units 23–24, section 4, 'Religion and working-class life'.)

Hymns can be taken as testimony for many things. Their texts, for example, reveal attitudes to various parts of the scripture, their music often hints at the formality or informality of the rituals in which they are used. The main factor that militates against making cut-and-dried statements about the entire hymn repertory of any given denomination is that, as we have seen, several hymn tunes in the nineteenth century were popular in several denominations.

But undoubtedly there were differences in the way that hymns were sung in different churches and chapels, certain 'performance conventions' were adopted that were appropriate to the ambience of the ritual of each denomination. For example, it would be surprising if there were no easily recognizable differences between the rendering of a hymn sung at a cathedral choral evensong and the same hymn sung in a Salvation Army citadel in the late nineteenth century. We can only guess at the precise identity of such conventions (though documentary records provide several clues) but hymns which have their origin in a particular denomination, a particular brand of conformity or nonconformity, often carry the flavour and the mood, the unwritten conventions of the act of worship.

Exercise

Please will you now listen to 'Sanctus' ('Glân Geriwbiaid a Seraffiaid'), 'Our Christian Band' and 'We'll be Heroes' (Cassette 5, side 1, band 2g, 2i, 2k). The first is a Welsh Nonconformist hymn by John Richards (his bardic name was Isalaw). The second, 'Our Christian Band', is by Ira Sankey and the third, 'We'll be Heroes', has been popular with the Salvation Army since the nineteenth century. As you listen to them I'd like you to jot down any features that strike you about them. Note, for example (1) the mood they evoke; (2) any musical features that are used which make them interesting.

Discussion

In my view, the feature that characterizes each of these hymns is that they are full-blooded and (dare I say it) *fun* to sing. In different ways they invite an enthusiastic congregational involvement.

'Sanctus'. This contains a great deal of variety of 'texture'; it is dramatic yet it is sufficiently straightforward to be genuinely congregational. It is in three sections that correspond to lines 1–4, 5–7 and line 8 of the text. The first four lines achieve effect by alternating unison (line 1 and 3) with harmony (line 2 and 4). The second section has a thick, close harmony which builds up to a pause (sustained note) on the last word of the penultimate line of each verse, then the dramatic, almost operatic chorus type setting of the repeated '*sanctaidd*' (holy) of the last line.

'Our Christian Band'. The point that strikes me most strongly about this hymn is the secular feel that it has. If the words were changed, the music could work neatly as a light music-hall song. The hymn has two sections – a verse and a chorus. In the verse, there is a type of call and response treatment reminiscent of certain types of light song. The chorus has a simple melodic line and harmonic treatment that makes it difficult to avoid joining in with.

'We'll be Heroes'. The tune here is simple enough but the lower (men's) voices move in a more decorative way. The really striking feature of this hymn is the extent to which it illustrates the spirit of the Salvationist military metaphor. It's a truly inspiring hymn and finds easy accord with Booth's maxim that was quoted earlier, 'Let it be a good tune . . . let us have a real tune . . . that one can take hold of, which people can learn, nay which *makes* them learn it' (italics added).

3.8 CONCLUSION

Comparing our examples of gospel song with, say, those characteristic of high church Anglicans heard earlier, it is often possible to see links between the religious views and practices of a group on the one hand and its favoured musical styles on the other. At the same time, it is important to remember the degree of musical consensus that developed in the 'middle ground' of Victorian society. And – a final point – unexpected connections could sometimes appear. The re-born English Catholic church cultivated a 'popular' style of hymn tune very similar to that of gospel song, despite the fact that the Catholics and the extreme revivalist and Evangelical groups were at opposite ends of the doctrinal and liturgical spectrum. Musical and religious choices do not always complement each other in an obvious way. The explanation in this case is probably that for both groups hymns were primarily a tool to win converts and retain adherents among the working classes rather than a cultural form whose language itself had religious and social significance.

4 CHALLENGES TO ORTHODOXY FROM WITHIN THE CHURCH

As we noted in the conclusion to section 2, 'The varieties of Victorian religion', by 1850 traditional Christian belief was already facing a challenge on both moral and scientific grounds, and, for a significant number of mid-Victorian intellectuals, a crisis of faith was already a reality. In 1859 Charles Darwin's *Origin of Species* was published and the ensuing controversy, over the implications of evolution and the theory of natural selection for religious belief, has been popularly understood to have been *the* great religious controversy of the Victorian age.

Section 5 of this unit will examine the actual impact of Darwin's ideas on Victorian religion. But for most mid-Victorian churchgoers, and certainly for most Anglicans, it was not *Origin of Species*, but a collection of essays innocuously entitled *Essays and Reviews* and published in February 1860, some months after *Origin of Species*, which posed the greatest threat to religious belief and became the focus of the greatest religious and theological controversy of the mid-Victorian era. Indeed, the Archbishop of Canterbury said in 1864 that no graver matter since the Reformation or in the next 200 or 300 years could be imagined.

Essays and Reviews consisted of seven essays on theological subjects, each by a different author, each of the authors being Anglican, one a layman and the other six clergymen. The authors and their essays were a mixed group in many respects. Their common ground was a commitment to a liberal and critical approach to Christian belief, the Bible and Christian doctrine. In this they represented the Broad Church or liberal tradition in Victorian Anglicanism – that is, a tradition occupying a theological position between the 'Low Church' Evangelicals and the 'High Church' Anglo-Catholics, heirs of the Oxford Movement.

As the preface to the book indicated, each of the seven essayists who contributed to *Essays and Reviews* was responsible for his own essay alone. It was intended by the authors as a collection of individual pieces of work. They did, however, include in the prefatory note the hope that the essays would be accepted 'as an attempt to illustrate the advantage derivable to the cause of religious and moral truth, from a free handling, in a becoming spirit, of subjects peculiarly liable to suffer by the repetition of conventional language and from traditional methods of treatment'. They sought, especially, to bring the new awareness of critical historical methods to bear upon the study of the Bible and the church's tradition. In this, they both explicitly and implicitly tried to introduce to Britain ideas about historical and biblical scholarship which were already common in Germany but were little known in this country in 1860.

The first essay was by Frederick Temple, then headmaster of Rugby school. Under the title 'The Education of the World', he argued that mankind had become sufficiently adult to study the Bible in a way which accepted scientific and literary criticism. In the second essay, on 'Bunsen's Biblical Researches', Rowland Williams, vice-principal and professor of Hebrew at St David's College, Lampeter, reviewed the work and implications of German critical scholarship on the Bible. Baden Powell, professor of Geometry at Oxford (and father of the founder of the Boy Scouts), wrote 'On the Study of the Evidences of Christianity' but concentrated on the theme of science, religion and the idea of the miraculous. The fourth essay, by Henry Wilson, a parish clergyman, was on 'The National Church' and discussed the nature of an established church, its limits and its comprehensiveness, stressing the moral quality of Christian life rather than doctrinal orthodoxy. Charles Goodwin, the one layman, wrote the fifth essay 'On the Mosaic Cosmogony' discussing the relationship between geological study and discoveries and the accounts of the creation in Genesis. Essay number six, by Mark Pattison, a tutor at Lincoln College, Oxford, was entitled 'Tendencies of

Religious Thought in England 1688–1750'. The final essay, by Benjamin Jowett, tutor at Balliol College and Professor of Greek at Oxford University, was concerned with the appropriate approach to the biblical text and entitled simply 'On the Interpretation of Scripture'.

The book caused an enormous furore. In five years it went into thirteen editions, and over 400 books, pamphlets and articles were written in reply to it. It was condemned by the bishops of the Church of England in 1861 and two of the authors, Rowland Williams and Henry Wilson, were charged with heresy and found guilty by the Ecclesiastical Court (though both were subsequently acquitted on appeal to the judicial committee of the Privy Council in 1864). The entire book was also 'synodically condemned' by the convocation of Canterbury and made the subject of a declaration, affirming all that it questioned, which was signed by 10,906 Anglican clergy in England, Wales and Ireland – just under half the Anglican clergy in those provinces of the church.

Why was it that this collection of essays caused so great a controversy? One answer to that question is, quite simply, that the challenges to certain traditional Christian beliefs from science, or from non-believing philosophers, or from morally critical thinkers and writers, could be dismissed by orthodox believers as merely the incomprehension or misunderstanding of outsiders (though such a dismissal was as unfounded as it was unwise). Here, however, criticism and doubt over certain orthodox beliefs came from *inside* the church, from clergy, from leading theologians – from men, that is to say, who understood traditional beliefs only too well and could not, therefore, simply be dismissed as uncomprehending or misinformed.

But what, specifically, caused the controversy? *Essays and Reviews* ran to over 400 pages and we cannot attempt to summarize the essays here. The following short quotations from each essay, however, illustrate points at which the authors offended the views of traditional believers.

 Exercise

Read through the following quotations and note those emphases which you think likely to have angered or offended traditional believers in the context of mid-Victorian Britain. This is not an easy exercise, partly because you have only short quotations on which to base your answers and, also, because you do not have available a precise definition of traditional belief. In the latter you are not alone. One of the recurrent problems facing historians of religious belief is precisely that of definition: the shape of Victorian orthodoxy is not an easy matter to set down. That said, I think it is possible to identify themes in these quotations which would be likely to offend traditional believers.

1. If geology proves to us that we must not interpret the first chapters of Genesis literally; if historical investigations shall show us that inspiration, however it may protect the doctrine, yet was not empowered to protect the narrative of the inspired writers from occasional inaccuracy... the results should be welcome. (Frederick Temple, 'The Education of the World')

2. We cannot encourage a remorseless criticism of Gentile histories and escape its contagion when we approach Hebrew annals... Thus considerations, religious and moral, no less than scientific and critical, have, where discussion was free, widened the area of Revelation for the old world and deepened it for ourselves; not removing the footsteps of the Eternal from Palestine, but tracing them on other shores; and not making the saints of old orphans, but ourselves partakers of their worship... The moral constituents of our nature, so often contrasted with Revelation, should rather be considered parts of its instrumentality. (Rowland Williams, 'Bunsen's Biblical Researches')

3. The boundaries of nature exist only where our *present* knowledge places them; the discoveries of tomorrow will alter and enlarge them. The inevitable progress of research must, within a longer or shorter period, unravel all that seems most marvellous, and what is at present least understood will become as familiarly known to

the science of the future as those points which a few centuries ago were involved in equal obscurity, but are now thoroughly understood. (Baden Powell, 'On the Study of the Evidences of Christianity')

4 Jesus Christ has not revealed His religion as a theology of the intellect, nor as an historical faith; and it is a stifling of the true Christian life, both in the individual and in the Church, to require of many men a unanimity in speculative doctrine, which is unattainable, and a uniformity of historical belief, which can never exist. (Henry Wilson, 'The National Church')

5 Physical science goes on unconcernedly pursuing its own path. Theology, the science whose object is the dealings of God with man as a moral being, maintains but a shivering existence, shouldered and jostled by the sturdy growths of modern thought, and bemoaning itself for the hostility which it encounters. Why should this be, unless because theologians persist in clinging to theories of God's procedure towards man, which have long been seen to be untenable? If, relinquishing theories, they would be content to enquire from the history of man what this procedure has actually been, the so-called difficulties of theology would, for the most part, vanish of themselves. (Charles Goodwin, 'On the Mosaic Cosmogony')

6 Whoever would take the religious literature of the present day as a whole, and endeavour to make out clearly on what basis Revelation is supposed by it to rest, whether on Authority, on the Inward Light, Reason, self-evidencing Scripture, or on the combination of the four, or some of them, and in what proportions, would probably find that he had undertaken a perplexing but not altogether profitless enquiry. (Mark Pattison, 'Tendencies of Religious Thought in England 1688–1750')

7 As the time has come when it is no longer possible to ignore the results of criticism, it is of importance that Christianity should be seen to be in harmony with them. That objections to some received views should be valid, and yet that they should be always held up as the objections of infidels, is a mischief to the Christian cause ... It would be a strange and incredible thing that the Gospel, which at first made war only on the vices of mankind, should now be opposed to one of the highest and rarest of human virtues – the love of truth.

... that in the present day the great object of Christianity would be, not to change the lives of men, but to prevent them from changing their opinions; that would be a singular inversion of the purposes for which Christ came into the world. *The Christian religion is in a false position when all the tendencies of knowledge are opposed to it...* No one can form any notion from what we see around us, of the power which Christianity might have if it were at one with the conscience of man, and not at variance with his intellectual convictions. (Benjamin Jowett, 'On the Interpretation of Scripture')

 Discussion

As I said earlier, this is not an easy exercise. It is also a very open one and you may well have grouped your answers differently from mine but still have identified many or all of the important points. My own way of arranging the points likely to offend traditional believers would be this:

1 The right, and the need, to approach the Bible critically is stressed by Temple, by Williams and by Jowett. The insights of geological and historical study should be welcome even if they challenge literal views of the Bible. There must be the same critical awareness of the Bible as an historical, human and therefore fallible source as there is of ancient gentile (i.e. Greek and Roman especially) historians and texts. Christianity must not ignore the results of historical criticism or it will oppose the highest of virtues, namely love of truth, and be at variance with current intellectual convictions.

2 Ideas of revelation (i.e. how God has revealed his existence and his purposes to humankind) should not be limited to the Bible and its traditions. There must be a recognition of 'revelation elsewhere' and of the role of conscience as part of, not opposed to, revelation (Williams). The question of where authority in religion lies is not a simple matter and the relationship of revelation, reason, scripture and inward experience is a perplexing subject (Pattison).

3 The advances of modern knowledge – whether in the study of the Bible (Jowett) or in physical science (Goodwin) or in the understanding of nature (Powell) – are such that theology must either revise its understanding of the ways of God to man or find itself in a false position, opposing the tendencies and progress of modern thought.

4 Wilson, in particular, objects that unanimity and uniformity of doctrine and belief are impossible, and argues that the true Christian *life* is stifled by the emphasis on such matters. This emphasis on the Christian life recurs in Goodwin's insistence on theology having to do primarily with the dealings of God with man as a *moral* being, and again in Jowett's stress upon the *moral* implications and demands of Christian belief.

5 Apart from specific points such as those suggested above, I think you would also be quite correct to suggest that there is a general spirit, or mood, of openness and acceptance towards modern thought, progress, science, criticism, and change in each of these writers. The mood might be expected to clash with those traditional believers whose faith stressed the unchanging, certain, and infallible nature of Christian belief. Similarly, the essayists' preference for natural, rather than miraculous, explanations of reality clashes with the miraculous and supernatural emphasis in traditional Christian belief.

The authors of *Essays and Reviews* shared a desire to reconcile Christianity with the critical scholarship and the leading intellectual tendencies – scientific, historical and moral – of their day. Hence they called for a thoroughly historical and critical approach to the Bible and for recognition of the moral and spiritual worth of sources and traditions other than the Bible. Hence also they sought acceptance of the findings of science concerning the age of the earth and its geological history, and concerning the possibility of miracles. They also argued for the recognition that the *moral* demands of the Christian *life* had a priority over dogma and doctrinal formulae.

The authors of *Essays and Reviews* also made more specific criticisms of traditional Christian beliefs. Williams for example argued that historical study of the Bible made it clear that the first five books of the Bible, traditionally held to be written by Moses, were in fact a complex compilation from many sources and by many authors. He also argued that the book of Isaiah contained the work of more than one prophet; that the book of Daniel was not contemporary history and belonged to the second not the sixth century BC and that prophecy in the Old Testament generally had a moral not predictive role: it was, he argued, meant to recall people to the moral life, not to predict the future.

Wilson similarly challenged specific doctrines by arguing that the word of God might be found in the Bible, but was not to be identified with the words of the Bible as such, and by suggesting that the idea of hell and eternal punishment might be morally dubious and that the Christian hope was better understood in terms of a universal salvation. Jowett meanwhile, in perhaps the single most notorious sentence in the book, directly challenged traditional views of scriptural authority by asserting that the only way in which the interpretation of scripture could meet the demands of critical historical understanding was to 'interpret the Bible like any other book'.

In point of fact, these various critical views put forward by the authors of *Essays and Reviews* were by no means startlingly new. Most of them had already been raised by the authors in articles, sermons and books, though in less sharply and starkly presented form, in the decade before the publication of *Essays and Reviews*. Three factors combined to create a major controversy in 1860. Firstly, the essayists were commonly held to have written with a self-consciously unified and critical aim. The writers, as we noted earlier, denied this, claiming in the preface that each was responsible only for his own contribution. Public opinion saw otherwise, however, and the denial of joint responsibility for the whole volume led only to accusations of conspiracy on the part of the authors. Secondly, the tone of the book was held to be unduly destructive and provocative: the authors, it was said, merely presented negative criticism, offering no positive substitute for that which they attacked. Finally, the book appeared to be addressed to the public rather than merely the academic community, as many of the authors' earlier expressions of such views had been. The public and popular aim of the essayists increased the concern of their opponents perhaps more than anything else.

Even then the controversy did not really get under way until the publication of an article by Frederic Harrison, a one-time High Churchman, but by 1860 a convinced atheist and secularist, in the *Westminster Review* for October 1860. The article was entitled 'Neo-Christianity' and censured the essayists for deserting historic Christianity but seeking to adapt and replace it with an unstable and hollow alternative, instead of frankly admitting disbelief. This article was followed in January 1861 by an equally hostile condemnation of the essayists in the *Quarterly Review* by Samuel Wilberforce, the Bishop of Oxford and self-appointed leader and co-ordinator of the clerical, and especially episcopal, opposition to the book. In response to these intensively hostile critics Arthur Stanley, a fellow Broadchurchman and Professor of Ecclesiastical History at Oxford, later to become Dean of Westminster, published an article in the *Edinburgh Review* of April 1861. Stanley defended the right of the essayists to speak as they did, though he by no means agreed with the content of all the essays.

These three long articles by Harrison, Wilberforce and Stanley were representative of the principal types of response to *Essays and Reviews* and demonstrate the issues which the mid-Victorian ecclesiastical and intellectual worlds felt to be at the centre of the controversy.

 Exercise

Please read the extracts from each of these articles in the Course Reader, extracts II.5, 6 and 7. The style of these articles is very dense and demanding, but I hope that by reading them, and the discussion of them which follows here, you will be able to sense the intensity with which the debate was conducted.

 Discussion

Frederic Harrison does not object to the liberalism of the essayists, to their use of historical and scientific criticism, evidence and argument, or to their academic conclusions over such matters as the possibility of miracles, the historical reliability of the Bible, or the status of doctrine. What he does object to are the failure to press these scientific and critical methods to their logical conclusions, and the attempt to portray the essayists' critical theological position as authentic historic Christianity, when it is obviously no such thing, in Harrison's view, but rather a new religion, a 'neo-Christianity'.

More specifically Harrison argues that the essays are in direct conflict with popular belief. Attempts to reconcile popular belief, especially popular Protestantism, with the views put forward in the essays are doomed to futility and end by being insincere. He ridicules the suggestion that orthodox Christianity can be saved from collapse by a series of revisions which effectively change its entire nature. He maintains that the public will never accept such a revision of Christianity but will see that the Bible and creeds in which they believe are simply undermined by this proposed defence.

In the end, the book, Harrison insists, challenges not merely specific points of doctrine but the very idea of doctrine as such. It seeks to avert the consequences of a clash between the modern intellect and religious belief by placing the moral element and the Christian life above the intellectual element and Christian belief.

Samuel Wilberforce is as forceful as Harrison in his opposition to the essayists. There can be no reconciliation, he argues, between the views of the essayists and the teaching of the Church of England. The essayists are claimed as allies by Harrison, an ardent atheist, and there is no clearer indication of their distance from historic Christianity than this common ground claimed by Harrison. The essayists omit from their proposed revision of Christian belief all the essentials of Christian faith. Their proposals are not merely a 'neo-Christianity' but rather a new religion altogether. Moreover, the proposal of such views is quite incompatible with the honest maintenance of the role of an Anglican clergyman.

The essayists also fail, Wilberforce maintains, to press their arguments to their final conclusions. They seek to criticize the biblical text and reject miracles and the supernatural whilst retaining the moral authority of the Bible and of Christian life and belief. In fact they should recognize that there cannot be any such rational middle way. They must accept a radical choice: either revelation, supernatural religion and miracle, or complete rationalism and the falsehood of Christianity.

The attempt to base a religion on morality and rationality is doomed to failure. Religious systems demand definite teaching, not merely moral precepts and noble sentiments, and because of this the Bible, creeds and revelation are the basis of Christianity. Take away these and you will also end in taking away the morality itself. Finally, the essayists simply exaggerate the extent to which traditional Christian belief, science, and modern knowledge are in conflict.

The third passage, from Arthur Stanley's article in the *Edinburgh Review*, stands in contrast to those of Harrison and Wilberforce. He criticizes those within the church, both Evangelical and Catholic – 'the partisans of the two chief theological schools in the country' – who eagerly take up arguments put forward by Harrison and use them to attack the essayists and thereby fuel the controversy. Long after the controversy has itself abated, Stanley argues, the questions which the essayists raise will remain: namely, the proper mode of interpreting scripture; the relative value in religion of internal evidence (experience and feeling) and external evidence (creed and dogma); and the relationship of dogmatic belief to the Bible and to history.

He particularly criticizes the various reviewers and critics of the essayists who have charged them with saying anything new – whether a 'neo-Christianity' or a new religion – and refers to the fact that, both in German theological writing and in Britain, the principles argued by the essayists have been known for fifty years. If there is a conspiracy, he argues, it is not on the part of the essayists alone but involves many of the leading clergy and bishops who have long known of these arguments.

Stanley also argues strongly that, contrary to the widespread demand for the withdrawal of these men from their positions as clergymen, they should stay within the church because their withdrawal would widen the gap between religion and science, devotion and truth, and the rising generation of intellectuals and the church. Also, he points out, the demand that they cease to be clergymen concentrates solely on the compatibility of their views with the formularies of the church, not on the truth or falsity of the views themselves. Stanley also suggests that within twenty years the essayists will not only be accepted but will occupy places of high responsibility in the church.

One aspect of these articles which I find particularly ironic is the similarity of argument and sympathy of opinion between the militant non-believer Harrison and the staunchly orthodox Bishop Wilberforce. For both non-believer and orthodox believer Christianity is to be defined in terms of supernaturalism, miracle, revelation, and dogma. The attempt to revise or reform Christian belief, in order to emphasize its moral dimensions and reconcile religious belief with modern knowledge, is ruled out as lacking in rigour (the essayists do not follow their arguments to their conclusions); dishonest (the essayists are trying to maintain a faith by changing it whereas they should simply acknowledge their disbelief); and doomed to failure (all religious systems need revelation and dogma and these proposals will not win popular approval).

Both unbeliever and bishop agree on the sharpness and absoluteness of the either/or nature of the argument. Either traditional Christianity or unbelief: the middle way is not a possibility.

4.1 EITHER/OR: ALL OR NOTHING

The controversy over *Essays and Reviews* does not merely reveal a good deal about the willingness of some mid-Victorian Christians to confront the challenges of scientific and historical scholarship and of moral criticism of traditional Christian beliefs. It also reveals much about the structure of traditional Christian belief in the 1860s.

It has been shown that among the many defences of traditional belief published in answer to *Essays and Reviews* a number of common points emerge. It is true that orthodox opponents of *Essays and Reviews* often differed in some of their specific arguments. Thus, for example, High Church writers frequently explained the unorthodoxy of the essayists as a reaction against the severity and intransigence of Evangelicalism, and stressed the importance of ecclesiastical authority and the tradition of the church as the basis of a reply to the essayists. On the other hand Evangelical opponents of the essayists often blamed what they considered to be the excesses of the Oxford Movement and its impact on the church for the position taken by the authors of *Essays and Reviews*.

Beyond such differences, however, a set of common arguments united the otherwise bitterly opposed Catholic and Evangelical parties against the essayists and their views. Just as the unbeliever Harrison and the orthodox Bishop Wilberforce made an 'unholy alliance' against the liberal essayists, so also High and Low Churchmen, Catholics and Evangelicals, made another 'unholy alliance' against a common perception of a threat to traditional Christian orthodoxy. The declaration against *Essays and Reviews* signed by almost 11,000 clergy was an excellent case in point. A declaration affirming belief in biblical inspiration and eternal punishment, it was organized by the veteran High Churchmen Pusey and Wilberforce and the Evangelical champion Lord Shaftesbury.

There were considerable differences amongst the opponents of the essayists over precisely *how* the Bible should be interpreted and what the inspiration of the Bible actually meant. But there was clear agreement that the essayists were quite wrong in their suggestions that divine inspiration applied only to the parts of the biblical text with a specifically religious or moral message and not to the narrative or historical or cosmological passages. The suggestions that the word of God was contained in, but not identical with, the biblical text, or that the Bible should be read 'like any other book' were equally strongly rejected. To the opponents of *Essays and Reviews* such arguments opened the door to limitless speculation, complete subjectivity of interpretation, and the loss of any objective standards for doctrine and belief. Once allow such criticisms and distinctions and where would it stop? Either the Bible must all be inspired and unique, or no certainty at all could be had.

A second common theme of the opponents of *Essays and Reviews* concerned their appeal to arguments based on the evidence which could be assembled to show the truth of Christianity. Taking up an eighteenth-century Anglican theological tradition, which was still deeply embedded in mid-Victorian Anglican theology, the opponents of *Essays and Reviews* argued that the evidence of miracles, the fulfilment of biblical prophecies and the fulfilment of Old Testament hopes and promises in the New Testament were conclusive evidence for the truth of Christianity, traditionally understood. *Essays and Reviews* had directly challenged both this whole approach to theology and each specific element in it. Powell had denied miracles; Williams had denied the predictive nature of the prophets; Jowett had rejected such a relationship between the texts of the Old and New Testaments; and Pattison, in his essay on the history of religious thought in England from 1688 to 1750, had put the eighteenth-century evidential theologians into a specific historical context.

Opponents of *Essays and Reviews*, including in this case non-believing critics like Frederic Harrison, also generally agreed on two other points. They were agreed that the critical views put forward by the essayists were out of step with popular Christian belief – out of step that is, not only in differing from popular Christianity, but also in being radically unacceptable to most people. They also agreed that the question of morality, and particularly the question of honesty, was central to the controversy. The morality and honesty of the essayists were attacked repeatedly. How could clergymen who had assented to the creeds and doctrinal formularies of the church honestly continue to hold their ecclesiastical posts and also criticize traditional belief in the way that they did? Surely the only honest position was to renounce their Christian belief and leave the church? It was, in effect, a moral version of the either/or argument: either you believed all of the traditional Christian position or you rejected it altogether; either you were morally honest in accepting Bible and creeds as traditionally understood, or you were morally honest in rejecting Christianity and leaving its offices, communities and practices. The 'honest doubter' was usually understood to be the agnostic who, accepting his or her doubts, stood apart from the church. The numbers of those who, like Stanley in his defence of the authors of *Essays and Reviews*, or like Tennyson in his conviction that 'There lives more faith in honest doubt/ Believe me, than in half the creeds', could conceive of honesty in the shape of critical faith and 'honest doubt' *within* the church were relatively few.

To the extent that it appeared to be the dominant ecclesiastical response to *Essays and Reviews* – as well as to other conflicts between religion and modern knowledge in the Victorian period – the either/or argument was a crucial element in the crisis of faith experienced by many mid-Victorian intellectuals. For many 'honest doubters' the final step out of some form of Christian belief was prompted not by the rise of new scientific or historical knowledge itself, but by the repeated insistence that Christian belief was all or nothing – a choice which, for many Victorian intellectuals, could have only one outcome: the relinquishing of Christian belief.

In other respects, especially within the church, the legacy of *Essays and Reviews*, and of the either/or argument, was not so clear. The judgement of the judicial committee of the Privy Council in 1864 acquitting Williams and Wilson of heresy meant that, however much bishops, clergy or laity might dislike it, Anglican clergy could hold views of the kind put forward in *Essays and Reviews*. One contemporary observer remarked satirically that the Privy Council acquittal of Williams and Wilson 'dismissed hell with costs, and took away from orthodox members of the Church of England their last hope of everlasting damnation'. Stanley's prediction that after 20 years the authors of *Essays and Reviews* would occupy high places in the church was fulfilled, up to a point. In 1869 Frederick Temple became Bishop of Exeter, subsequently becoming Bishop of London and finally, in 1897, Archbishop of Canterbury.

4.2 A MIDDLE WAY?

In 1889, at the very end of the period we are studying here, another volume of essays by Anglican clergy appeared. Entitled *Lux Mundi* and written by younger representatives of the Catholic wing of the Church of England, this collection of essays again challenged Christians to take seriously the findings of science and history and their implications for theology and for the study of the Bible. Again there was controversy, but nowhere near on the scale of that surrounding *Essays and Reviews*. Individual theologians and groups condemned *Lux Mundi*, but there were no prosecutions for heresy, no synodical or episcopal condemnations, and nothing like the public furore in the press. Thus far had the religious mood changed in the 25 years between 1864 and 1889.

And yet Stanley's hopes were also too sanguine and too optimistic. A careful comparison of *Essays and Reviews* with *Lux Mundi* reveals that whilst the later volume of essays is better constructed, better written and better edited, it is also, for all its attempts to accommodate a moderate historical and scientific worldview, a much safer, much less daring book than *Essays and Reviews*. *Essays and Reviews* offered the mid-Victorian church the opportunity to construct a full-blooded alternative to the traditional theology. That traditional theology was based on external evidences and intellectual assent to a body of given religious truths. In its place the essayists proposed a theological approach in which religious feeling and experience had priority over externally given doctrine and belief. Experience and feeling were on the one hand to be the means by which the enduring religious values of the Christian tradition and of the Bible were to be appropriated, and on the other hand they were also to be the basis of criticizing specific doctrines and beliefs which no longer corresponded to contemporary moral and religious intuition. Among morally questionable matters were, for example, the moral dubiousness of hell or the moral failure involved in denying modern knowledge in order to retain specific beliefs about creation, miracles and prophecy.

Lux Mundi adopted nothing like as radical an approach: rather, it sought a middle way between the radical proposals of the authors of *Essays and Reviews* and the traditional theology which they had opposed. Certainly there was room in the mid- and late Victorian context for a variety of approaches to the problem of religion and modern thought, and the mediating stance of *Lux Mundi* was one possible avenue, as was the staunch conservatism of more traditional Christians, both Evangelical and Catholic. The great irony of *Essays and Reviews* was that, despite the acquittal of Williams and Wilson and the episcopal career of Temple, the particular theological avenue opened by the essayists was not subsequently systematically explored and developed.

It has been said that *Essays and Reviews* was at once the culmination and the final act of the Broad Church tradition in Victorian Anglicanism. Certainly the radical theological tradition represented by the essayists did not make any comparable or concerted contribution to Victorian religious thought after *Essays and Reviews*, partly at least because they had been so bitterly opposed by so large a part of the religious establishment. Benjamin Jowett is perhaps the representative figure in this respect. It was agreed both at the time and by subsequent historians of the controversy that Jowett's essay 'On the Interpretation of Scripture' was the most profound of the contributions to *Essays and Reviews*. It was also generally acknowledged that of all the essayists, perhaps of all the Broad Churchmen, Jowett had the potential to work coherently through the religious and theological alternative which the essayists represented. In fact Jowett was so shocked and hurt by the intensity of the controversy over *Essays and Reviews* that he never again produced a major theological work, concentrating instead on his work as an Oxford college tutor, and later Master of Balliol, his classical studies and occasional religious and theological writings.

Later Victorian Christianity did become more open to historical and scientific scholarship. But to the extent that the controversy over *Essays and Reviews* discouraged theologians like Jowett from risking further controversy, the exponents of the either/or approach to religious belief ensured a deepening of the crisis of faith experienced by many mid- and late Victorian intellectuals and also contributed to the steady fragmentation of Victorian intellectual life whereby arts, science and religion came to be regarded as separate areas of cultural life, rather than, as in the early Victorian period, one aspect of a common cultural and intellectual context.

In the end, the impact of *Essays and Reviews* was probably greatest inside the church and among those intellectuals who, in the 1850s and 1860s, were still struggling to hold together Christian faith and modern thought. Within the church, despite *legal* judgement allowing greater freedom of opinion, the theological mood actually grew more conservative and traditional beliefs were stridently affirmed. For the 'honest doubters' the task of continuing to hold together Christian faith and modern thought became that much more difficult.

What *Essays and Reviews* did *not* do — and in this it shared common ground with Darwin's *Origin of Species* and the whole science and religion issue — was cause the spectacular absence from Christian worship of the majority of the working classes. That absence was the other great concern of the Victorian churches but, as we shall see in Units 23–24, the roots of that spectacular absence lay in the relationship between religion and class, not in the intellectual crises of mid-Victorian religious life.

5 CHALLENGES TO RELIGIOUS AUTHORITY FROM SCIENTISTS AND PHILOSOPHERS

5.1 THE CULT OF SCIENCE

Beatrice Webb, the writer and pioneer socialist, was a young woman during the 1870s and 1880s, living in an intellectual household. This is how she recalled those decades:

> In these latter days of deep disillusionment [i.e. the 1920s], now that we have learnt, by the bitter experience of the Great War, to what vile uses the methods and results of science may be put, when these are inspired and directed by brutal instinct and base motive, it is hard to understand the naïve belief of the most original and vigorous minds of the 'seventies and 'eighties that it was by science, and by science alone, that all human misery would be ultimately swept away. This almost fanatical faith was perhaps partly due to hero-worship. For who will deny that the men of science were the leading British intellectuals of that period; that it was they who stood out as men of genius with international reputations; and that it was they who were the self-confident militants of the period; that it was they who were routing the theologians, confounding the mystics, imposing their theories on philosophers, their inventions on capitalists, and their discoveries on medical men; whilst they were at the same time snubbing the artists, ignoring the poets and even casting doubts on the capacity of the politicians?
> (B. Webb, *My Apprenticeship*, pp.130–1)

Perhaps the most famous of this group of scientists whom Webb saw as dominating Victorian cultural life was T. H. Huxley, who routed Samuel Wilberforce, the Bishop of Oxford, in a public debate over Darwin's *Origin of Species*. (Wilberforce, as a leading conservative Anglican, was as keen to attack

Figure 4   Thomas Henry Huxley, cartoon by Ape, for Vanity Fair, *1871. (Source: Mansell Collection)*

Figure 5   Bishop Samuel Wilberforce, cartoon by Ape, for Vanity Fair, *1869. (Source: Mansell Collection)*

Units 18–19 Religion: Conformity and Controversy

Darwin's book as he was to attack *Essays and Reviews*.) Other members of the group that Beatrice Webb recalled will probably be less familiar to you, but they were eminent Victorians. There was Professor J. Tyndall, who used his presidential address to the British Association for the Advancement of Science in 1874 to say this:

> The impregnable position of science may be described in a few words. We claim, and we shall wrest, from theology the entire domain of cosmological theory. All schemes and systems which thus infringe upon the domain of science must, *in so far that they do this*, submit to its control, and relinquish all thought of controlling it. Acting otherwise proved disastrous in the past, and is simply fatuous today. (Quoted in Basalla et al., *Victorian Science*, pp.474–5)

And there was the statistician Professor K. Pearson, who, at the very end of our period, summed up the claims of science in his book *The Grammar of Science* (1892):

> Modern science does much more than demand that it shall be left in undisturbed possession of what the theologian and metaphysician please to term its 'legitimate field'. It claims that the whole range of phenomena, mental as well as physical – the entire universe – is its field. It asserts that the scientific method is the sole gateway to the whole region of knowledge. (Pearson, *The Grammar of Science*, pp.26–7)

Why did these men shout so assertively? Why were they so confident that theirs was the sole means of interpreting the universe?

Within the Christian tradition, limits had customarily been set on the domain of science. But such limits came to appear increasingly unreal and unacceptable as the nineteenth century wore on. People still wrote as if there were a proper domain for scientific investigation outside which science could claim no authority. In particular, it was common to find writers arguing that inquiries into the human mind or 'soul', into the history of the earth, and into the nature and origin of life, demanded the supplementary expertise of the Christian theologian. These attempts to set limits to the domain of science were openly opposed by 'advanced' thinkers of the sort that captivated the young Beatrice Webb. Pearson, in the passage that you've just read, claimed that *nothing* is beyond the domain of science.

He was a representative of a movement that had been developing, both in France and in Britain, which denied that there was any reality not open to scientific investigation – a movement known as 'Positivism'. The philosopher John Stuart Mill was a 'positivist' and his utilitarian ethics was quite expressly conceived as an alternative to the conventional, religiously sanctioned morality of his day. For Mill, both the study of human nature and even of morality could be put on an agreed scientific basis quite independent of religion.

The idea of a special part of human beings (the 'soul') which is the province of religion and not of science is a very familiar one. It still finds its defenders today. It had not gone without challenge in the eighteenth century, especially in France, where intellectuals assailed the authority of the Roman Catholic Church. And it was challenged again in nineteenth-century Britain by some of the more 'advanced' Victorians. One such was W. K. Clifford, Professor of Applied Mathematics at University College London. Clifford was not a philosopher of Mill's stature but was drawn into philosophical writing by the general claims he made on behalf of 'the domain of Science' and through the general conclusions about human beings to which he was led through reflection on the results of scientific inquiry. The 'domain of Science' extended, according to Clifford, to 'all possible human knowledge which can rightly be used to guide human conduct'. Like many of his contemporaries, Clifford professed agnosticism about the existence of God. At the same time he was confident that science could illuminate the mysteries about human nature which had previously been the preserve of religion.

5 Challenges to religious authority

 Exercise

I suggest you now read the extract from Clifford's lecture 'Body and Mind', originally delivered to the Sunday Lecture Society in 1874, and reprinted in the Course Reader (extract II.10). Note, incidentally, that Clifford gave his lecture on a Sunday. This would certainly have affronted the pious. It was as if he were delivering an alternative, secular, sermon. When you have read the extract, please make a note of your answer to these questions:

1 What alternative does Clifford offer to a religious view of human beings?
2 What alternative does Clifford offer to a religious view of morality?

 Discussion

1 Clifford denies the existence of 'consciousness apart from a nervous system, of mind without a body'. He denies, therefore, the separate existence of a mind or soul for which immortality might be claimed and which might therefore be claimed to belong within the domain of religion.

2 Clifford insists that 'the only right motive to right action is to be found in the social instincts which have been bred into mankind by hundreds of generations of social life'. Morality does not, according to Clifford, need to be understood by supposing humans to have a divinely-inspired 'voice' or conscience. 'The distinction of right and wrong grows up in the broad light of day out of natural causes...'

There were doubtless many in the nineteenth century who continued to believe that a division between scientific and religious authority could still be maintained. But philosophers, and scientists, by and large, found such a compromise unconvincing.

5.2 THE SCIENTISTS' BID FOR CULTURAL SUPREMACY

So far, you have been looking, in the work of Clifford, Tyndall, Pearson and Mill, at intellectual challenges to religious authority. But the challenge of thinkers like these had another, much more public, dimension. You will recall that Clifford gave his lecture on a Sunday. By so doing he was making a point about the subtle but powerful grip that churches exerted over public life in Britain. It is to the public dimension of the philosophers' and scientists' challenge that we'll now turn.

The sheer stridency of their writing was due largely to the confidence with which they could point to the successes of science. Scientific knowledge had increased spectacularly during the nineteenth century, and scientists were proud. More and more of the workings of the universe had been marshalled under scientific laws. Science was enjoying a vogue in the nation at large. The middle classes botanized and geologized earnestly, scientific lecturers could fill evening classes at Mechanics' Institutes with rows of orderly artisans waiting to hear about the wonders of electricity, and the popular magazines were loaded with often very demanding scientific articles. Science was beginning to exert an influence in areas of cultural life that had formerly been the preserve of religion.

However, these changes in the fortunes of science and religion had not been accompanied by any equivalent changes in scientific and religious *institutions*. For example, science occupied still only a very marginal place in British education. Not until 1886 was it possible at Oxford University to bypass large doses of compulsory classics and take a specialized science degree. And there were few jobs for professional scientists. Men like Tyndall and Huxley, who had no great personal fortunes, had to struggle to make a living. Darwin, the greatest biologist of the century, never held a university post, received no research grants, and worked at home, supported by a private income. At the same time, the Church of England had an established stake in national life: it dominated Oxford and Cambridge universities, and its bishops sat in the House of Lords. This imbalance in the prestige of science and religion, as *institutions,* made scientists – especially young and needy scientists – loudly proclaim the importance of their calling.

Lastly, the fervour of the scientists' claim derived from their belief that science somehow embodied guarantees of inevitable progress. 'Progress' was a Victorian watchword. It was never sharply defined, but in the writings of the philosopher and sociologist, Herbert Spencer, it was made to sound as reassuring as the religion it replaced. The Bible may be a mere collection of fables; religious observance might be a pantomime, but in science, the earnest Victorian could find the hope that the universe was evolving onwards and upwards, and that at the very growing point of evolution stood the British, middle-class, male. Spencer had even tried to codify a *law* of progress:

> Progress . . . is not an accident, but a necessity. Instead of civilization being artificial, it is a part of nature; all of a piece with the development of the embryo or the unfolding of a flower. The modifications mankind have undergone, and are still undergoing, result from a law underlying the whole organic creation; and provided the human race continues, and the constitution of things remains the same, those modifications must end in completeness. As surely as the tree becomes bulky when it stands alone, and slender if one of a group . . . as surely as a blacksmith's arm grows large, and the skin of a labourer's hand thick . . . so surely must the human faculties be moulded into complete fitness for the social state; so surely must the things we call evil and immorality disappear; so surely must man become perfect. (Spencer, *Social Statics.* Quoted in Peel, *Herbert Spencer, the Evolution of a Naturalist,* p.101)

Spencer's writings captivated the young Beatrice Webb, and many like her, who had rejected formal religion yet still wanted hope and reassurance. She was not to be put off by her father's opinion of Spencer's philosophizing: 'words, my dear, mere words'. But Beatrice's father was right: science does not discover a law of progress, and a few of those scientists who applauded Spencer's general advocacy of their activities had grave reservations about his vague notions of progress. Darwin and Huxley, notably, came to see that evolution does not guarantee progress, however that term is defined. And in a larger sense, and as Beatrice Webb sadly noted later, the First World War put a painful end to beliefs in the inevitability of progress.

But during our period, many scientists and philosophers were unabashed. You can see them in action if we look at one episode in their bid for cultural supremacy.

5.3 THE PRAYER GAUGE DEBATE

The practice of the church had, for centuries, been to encourage Christians to believe that prayers, sincerely uttered, can materially affect the course of events. Prayers for the sick, for good harvests, or for relief from bad weather, were routine in all parishes. Some Christian thinkers had taken a different view of prayer: they argued that the object of prayer was not to change the course of material events, but to bring the person who prayed into a state of grace. But the predominant view amongst both clergy and their congregations at the beginning of our period was that prayer can elicit from God a practical response: the sick might be cured; the weather might change.

Now, in a period in which a group of energetic scientists were eager to displace religious authority and replace it with their own, and believed that the natural order is governed by scientific laws whose working cannot be altered by human supplication, prayer was a productive battleground, and throughout the period from 1850 to 1890, a straggling and inconclusive argument about the efficacy of prayer went back and forth. The history of the debate about the efficacy of prayer has been researched and written up by F. M. Turner and my discussion closely follows his article (Turner, 'Rainfall, plagues and the Prince of Wales: a chapter in the conflict of religion and science').

Four times, between 1831 and 1849, the Privy Council had sanctioned special days of prayer for relief from cholera. But in 1853, the Prime Minister, Lord Palmerston, turned down a request from the Presbytery of Edinburgh to appoint a fast day to keep cholera at bay. Palmerston's reason for this change was his belief that the causes of cholera were now supposed to be understood by scientists, and that, as a consequence, sanitation, rather than prayer, was the answer. The point here is that as scientific explanations for misfortunes became available, prayer perhaps tended to become obsolete. But Palmerston's rejection of prayer and fasting did not establish a pattern of decreasing national reliance on prayer. Orthodox bishops fought hard to keep the practice alive. They believed wholeheartedly in the efficacy of prayer. As its national co-ordinators, they had also a professional stake in the matter.

In 1860, the Bishop of Oxford – Darwin's, Huxley's and the liberal theologian's old antagonist – and other bishops instructed their clergy to institute prayers for fine weather. There was doubt in the Bishop of Oxford's mind neither about the cause of the bad weather, nor about the way to change it. As he wrote to his clergy, 'The time appears to me to have come when the continuance of wet weather, by preventing the gathering of the fruits of the earth in this season, may be considered as one of the judgements of Almighty God, to be averted by our humble prayers and intercessions' (Turner, 'Rainfalls, plagues and the Prince of Wales ...').

Five years later, in 1865, the rivalry between the scientists and the traditional clergy surfaced. The occasion was an outbreak of cattle plague. The physical cause of this plague was unknown. The government appointed a Royal Commission under the zealous scientist Lyon Playfair, and soon the cattle trade was regulated. Preventive slaughtering of beasts was carried out. Meanwhile, the Archbishop of Canterbury issued a prayer:

> Oh Lord God Almighty, whose are the cattle on a thousand hills, and in whose hand is the breath of every living thing, look down, we pray Thee, in compassion upon us Thy servants, whom Thou hast visited with a grievous murrain among our herds and flocks. We acknowledge our transgressions, which worthily deserve Thy chastisement, and our sin is ever before us; and in humble penitence we do come to seek Thy aid. In the midst of judgement do Thou, O Lord, remember mercy; stay, we pray Thee, this plague by Thy word of power, and save that provision which Thou hadst in Thy goodness granted for our sustenance. Defend us also, gracious Lord, from the pestilence with which many foreign lands have been smitten; keep it, we beseech Thee, far away from our borders, and shield our homes from its ravages; so shall we ever offer unto Thee the sacrifice of praise and thanksgiving, for these Thy acts of providence over us, through Jesus Christ our Lord. Amen. (Turner, 'Rainfalls, plagues and the Prince of Wales ...')

This prayer was approved by the Privy Council and went out to the parishes. (Note, incidentally, that it asks God to keep the plague away only from Britain's borders: presumably those in foreign lands that had been smitten could pray for themselves.) The prayer brought Professor John Tyndall – who, you will recall, proclaimed that schemes that infringe upon the domain of science must 'submit to its control' – and Lyon Playfair – the head of the commission into the disease – into action with letters published in the great forum of Victorian public debate, the monthly journals. Tyndall and Playfair argued that prayer would not affect the course of the cattle plague, but that scientific research very well might do so. It is plain though, that what was at issue here was not just the life and death of the nation's cows, but the authority of its cultural leaders. To whom should troubled people turn; their clergymen or scientific experts?

The next episode concerned not cattle or fine weather, but the heir to the throne. In December 1871, the Prince of Wales caught typhoid. The best doctors were unable to cure him. Medical science was not up to the task. The government, in consultation with the bishops, issued orders to the clergy: Sunday 10 December was designated a national day of prayer for the Prince's recovery. On the following Thursday, the Prince took a turn for the better. At once, the incident was taken up by defenders and attackers of the power of prayer. One defender, the Revd. W. Karslake, preached a sermon on 'God's answer to a nation's prayer'. The medical and scientific community were, it seemed, routed. The efficacy of prayer had been demonstrated. The rout was completed when doctors and scientists were conspicuously excluded from the invitation list to the service of thanksgiving at St Paul's Cathedral that followed the Prince's recovery. (An interesting local manifestation of this rejoicing was the commissioning of a Pre-Raphaelite stained-glass window for St Martin-on-the-Hill, Scarborough. See Figure 6.)

But the scientists struck back in 1872 with a neat and deliberately impious challenge. Tyndall and a London surgeon, Henry Thompson, declared that the whole question of the efficacy of prayer could be settled by an experiment. They proposed that one hospital ward containing patients with well understood diseases be singled out. Its patients should then systematically be prayed for by all Christians for about three to five years. The recovery rate in this ward could then be compared with recovery rates of patients with the same diseases but who had been treated in wards that had not been subjected to this intensive prayer. If prayer works, they concluded, there should be a differential recovery rate. The experiment offered Christians, as Thompson wickedly concluded, 'an occasion of demonstrating to the faithless an imperishable record of the real power of prayer'. The experiment would establish a 'Prayer Gauge'. As might be expected, the challenge was not taken up. Bishops were not going to fight on the terms of their opponents. We needn't follow the ins and outs of the debate any further. But if you couple it with your reading of the Clifford extract, you should find that some important features of Victorian intellectual and cultural life have been established.

First, during the Victorian period, there was the possibility of debate between scientists, philosophers and clergymen. (And, it might be added, poets. The Poet

Figure 6   Stained-glass window in St Martin-on-the-Hill, Scarborough, depicting St Peter, St Stephen and St Paul. Designed by Edward Burne-Jones and commissioned by the church's benefactor, Mary Craven. The wording is 'A thank offering for the recovery of the Prince of Wales 1872 by Mary Craven'. (Photo: P. H. K. Smith)

Laureate, Tennyson, was, as you will see later, perfectly alert to, and actively engaged in, the sorts of debates we've been looking at.) They were products of a single, unified culture. They understood each other perfectly. But they were at a parting of the ways. In particular, Britain would not much longer have a culture that harmonized religion and science. The two enterprises were to take different routes, and lose both the interest in, and the possibility of, discussing fundamental issues before the public. As you have already seen, the debate over *Essays and Reviews,* fought out in the same forum – the monthly and quarterly journals – was part of this process of cultural fragmentation.

Secondly, although there were plainly matters of deep conviction at stake, behind these convictions lurked concerns about professional status and cultural leadership. Young scientists dreamed of ultimately replacing the Christian priesthood with a scientific priesthood.

And finally, during the Victorian period, scientists loudly and confidently laid claim to the whole universe, mental and physical, as their domain, and demanded further that, within that domain, they alone could establish what would count as knowledge.

5.4 CHARLES DARWIN

The scientist who most profoundly affected Victorian religion does not, at first sight, exhibit the characteristics that we have just established. He had virtually no public life. He never once defended his theory of evolution in public. He never gave a lecture on evolution. He had no job and didn't want one: he was rich enough to do without. He always tried not to give offence to people's religious feelings, and he never overtly made the great sweeping claims for science that Clifford, Pearson and Huxley made. But in a powerful sense, he was part of their movement – indeed, was one of its founding fathers. This is how Francis Galton, a pioneer statistician, and, in the eyes of the young Beatrice Webb, the very epitome of the Victorian Man of Science, described the impact that reading Darwin's *Origin of Species* had had on him:

> The publication in 1859 of the *Origin of Species* by Charles Darwin made a marked epoch in my own mental development, as it did in that of human thought generally. Its effect was to demolish a multitude of dogmatic barriers by a single stroke, and to arouse a spirit of rebellion against all ancient authorities whose positive and unauthenticated statements were contradicted by modern science. (Galton, *Memories of my life.* Quoted in Forrest, *Francis Galton.*)

In a restrained, but quietly insistent way, Darwin was extending the domain of science – was offering an account of the origin of species, including the human species and the human mind, that left no place for the hand of God.

To understand Darwin, we have to go back to beyond the beginning of our period, to the 1840s. In 1844, in a diffident, guarded letter to a friend, Charles Darwin wrote 'At last gleams of light have come, and I am almost convinced (quite contrary to the opinion I started with) that species are not (it is like confessing a murder) immutable.' In this halting sentence, Darwin announced to his friend that he had formulated a theory to account for the origin of species. He did not elaborate the theory in this letter, nor in any other that he wrote at the time. He kept his theory dark, giving away few details, even to close scientific colleagues. Working in virtual seclusion at his home in Kent, he spent a further fifteen years in getting the theory into a form suitable for presentation to a critical, probably hostile public. In 1859, he was finally prodded into publishing his theory and he issued it as *On the Origin of Species by Means of Natural Selection.*

Just as he had predicted, his book at once drew forth some fierce denunciations. The *Origin* said very little directly about the origin of the human species, but Darwin had clearly implied that humans, like every other species, have descended from earlier species. Here is how Samuel Wilberforce, the Bishop of Oxford, responded to the proposal that humans are descended from the brutes. The extract comes from a review of the *Origin* that Wilberforce wrote for the Tory *Quarterly Review*.

> Man's derived supremacy over the earth; man's power of articulate speech; man's gift of reason; man's free-will and responsibility; man's fall and man's redemption; the incarnation of the Eternal Son; the indwelling of the Eternal Spirit – all are equally and utterly irreconcilable with the degrading notion of the brute origin of him who was created in the image of God, and redeemed by the Eternal Son assuming to himself his nature.

The Bishop was making very plain his conviction that Darwin's theory was 'utterly irreconcilable' with some of the central propositions of Christianity. Darwin had seen this coming. He knew full well that although his theory was addressed strictly to the biological problem of how species have come into existence, no matter how carefully he handled it, his book would strike at the heart of Christian belief. It was this knowledge that had made him say, when he privately announced the theory to his friend, that it was like 'confessing a murder'.

The aspect of Darwin's theory that the Bishop of Oxford most disliked was the assertion of the descent of humans from the brutes, and it was this aspect that lodged most prominently in the Victorian public imagination, and which most spectacularly affronted the biblical account of human origins. But Darwin's theory had another aspect, an aspect that was just as difficult to reconcile with Christian beliefs about how the world is ordered. Darwin proposed not just that species have evolved, but that the mechanism that drives the process along is 'natural selection'.

As Darwin formulated it, the theory of natural selection works like this. It is a common observation that there is never enough food to sustain every animal that is born, or seed that germinates. There is always, in Darwin's phrase, 'a struggle for existence'. Now, in any population of plants or animals, those individuals that exhibit variations – in height, colour, speed, for example – that confer on them an advantage, however slight, in the struggle for existence – in the hunt for food, or in escaping predators, for instance – will be 'naturally selected'. That is to say, they will survive and breed. And since offspring tend to resemble their parents, the parents' advantageous, adaptive variations will be transmitted from generation to generation. On the other hand, those individuals whose variations place them at a disadvantage in the struggle for existence will be weeded out, will die before breeding. To use the phrase that became indissolubly linked to Darwin's theory, it is a matter of 'the survival of the fittest'. If environmental conditions start to change, those individuals best adapted to the changing conditions will be naturally selected. As a result, over thousands of generations, the overall character of the population will alter: a new variety, and eventually a new species, will be in the process of evolving.

For our purposes, one point about the processes of natural selection and the survival of the fittest is important: they do not look like the sort of processes that a good and wise god would have ordained for the management of his creation. They depend on struggle, chance, and waste. As Darwin, in one of his blacker moods, confided, in a letter to a friend: 'What a book a devil's chaplain might write on the clumsy, wasteful, blundering, low, and horribly cruel works of nature!'

Darwin's theory, then, presented three challenges to Christians. The first challenge was implicit, but perfectly clear. The *Origin of Species* implied that the biblical account of creation is wrong. Species of plants and animals have not been divinely and individually created: they have evolved. Secondly, the mechanism that drives evolution along is a mechanism of waste and struggle. Thirdly, this mechanism of natural selection is sufficient to account for the emergence of humans: no special case, requiring perhaps the hand of God, needs to be made out to account for the emergence and characteristics of the human race.

5.5 THE DARWINIAN DEBATES

The challenge was met in a variety of ways, but before we look at some of them, three important points about the character of the Darwinian debates need to be made. First, although Darwin raised issues whose reverberations are still strongly sounding, it is difficult to say how great an influence he had on Victorian religious life as a whole. There were sermons in which he was discussed; there were public debates; numbers of individuals testified that *Origin of Species* had demolished their faith. But Darwin didn't single-handedly empty the pews. As Gerald Parsons remarked in the last section, in any list of causes of decline in church attendance, loss of faith as a consequence of reading *Origin of Species* will be pretty low down.

Secondly, the Darwinian debates were accessible to all educated Victorians. Of course, there were specialist scientific societies and periodicals, and there were specialist religious periodicals, but scientific and religious issues were regularly aired before a wide general public. The denunciation of Darwin's theory by the Bishop of Oxford that you have just read is a good example of the public airing of a complex and detailed issue. The extract comes from a long article that the Bishop wrote for one of the most influential general periodicals of the time, the *Quarterly Review*. Readers of the *Quarterly*, and of many other Victorian journals, would typically find long, demanding articles on science, history, politics, economics, religion, art and literature. A single issue might well contain detailed articles on Darwin's theory and on *Essays and Reviews*, for example. Victorian educated opinion was remarkably integrated: notably, there was no division between 'arts' and 'science' – a division that we now take almost for granted. We have already suggested that the slow fragmentation of what one writer has called this 'common context' of Victorian intellectual life is one of the most important long-term cultural changes in the period we are studying.

Thirdly, the Darwinian debates had a poignancy and tension that derived from a peculiar tradition in British science. Since the seventeenth century, scientists had commonly seen their enterprise as one that automatically showed the universe to have been designed by a good god who had exquisitely adapted his creation to the needs of his creatures. As science advanced, reverence for God advanced alongside. Scientific knowledge was knowledge of God's brilliant handiwork. With some notable exceptions, British scientists were supporters of religion, not its enemies. Indeed, there was often no sharp distinction between a man's science and his religion: some of the best scientists, especially in geology and biology, were clergymen. This characteristic of British science comes out in the following passage, which is from the first issue of the *Zoological Journal*:

> The contemplation of the works of the creation necessarily leads the mind to that of the Creator himself – and the more intimate our acquaintance with the former, the deeper and more devoted will be our adoration of the great author of all things! . . . [The naturalist] sees the beautiful connection that subsists throughout the whole scheme of animated nature. He traces, from the bulk and strength of the massive elephant to the almost invisible structure of the minutest insect, a mutual dependancy, that convinces him nothing is made in vain. He feels, too, that at the head of all this system of order and beauty, pre-eminent in the dominion of his reason, stands Man. He sees himself as the favoured creature of his Creator, and the finest energies of his soul are roused to gratitude and devotion. (*Zoological Journal*, Vol. I, 1824, p.vii)

This was published in 1824 and is typical of the tone of the biology and geology that the young Darwin was taught at Cambridge University. Darwin went to Cambridge intending to become a country clergyman. With a decent private income, and a trouble-free parish, he would, he imagined, be able quietly to pursue his investigations into beetles and publish the odd research article.

The poignancy of the Darwinian debates comes from the ironic source of the theory. It had been nourished by the very tradition that it would destroy. The desolate feeling of many scientists and clergymen who read the *Origin of Species* was that their universe had been snatched from them by – to use Darwin's private phrase – a devil's chaplain, and represented as the very opposite of what they had confidently believed. For example, biologists had traditionally singled out the eye as a plain demonstration of the skill of the creator: surely only God has the wisdom and foresight to design such an intricate and wonderful organ. Darwin, reared in this tradition, unerringly chose the eye as a test piece for his natural selection theory. In *Origin of Species*, he aimed to show that the organ could have been developed by the accumulation of naturally selected tiny variations: no heavenly superintendence of the process, he argued, was necessary.

We can now look at a few contributions to the debate that *Origin of Species* provoked.

5.6 THE RESPONSE TO DARWIN'S THEORY

Some readers, like the Bishop of Oxford, rejected the theory outright. Species, they maintained, have not evolved. These outright critics were able to mount a pretty impressive case against evolution. Where are the missing links between major groups of animals – say between birds and reptiles? How could entirely new features, like wings, for example, have evolved? What possible survival advantage would be conferred on an individual that varied only to the extent of having, say, only the rudiments of wings that weren't powerful enough to enable it actually to fly? Despite the most intensive work, domestic breeders have been unable to produce a new species: why should wild nature have been able to do more?

In anticipation of these, and other serious objections, Darwin had devoted a chapter of *Origin of Species* to the difficulties facing the theory, but his arguments were not decisive. The tactic that he fell back on, and which became a standard ploy of later Darwinians, was to ridicule the alternative to evolution. Evolution certainly has its problems, the Darwinians conceded, but who can take seriously the alternative proposition that millions of species have been miraculously created?

It was a shrewd move. Although outright critics could mount a pretty substantial scientific case against evolution, they were ultimately defending the biblical account of creation. And Darwinians believed that the exposure of what they saw as the incredibility of the Book of Genesis would give the theory of evolution an enhanced attractiveness. This strategy paid off. They were able to tap the growing feeling among educated opinion that the literal word of the Bible was of no use to biologists and geologists – the feeling that the writers of *Essays and Reviews* were trying to address. Evolution, problematic as it was, offered a way forward: the biblical account of creation was, to research scientists, a dead end.

Among the public at large, or perhaps just among unsophisticated Christian congregations, outright critics could make more headway, for there, people were readier to believe that the Bible is an infallible guide to earth history, and that if scientists propose otherwise, so much the worse for science.

In general then, members of the educated community who kept abreast of developments in biology, were persuaded by Darwin that species have evolved. The cumulative argument of *Origin of Species* was persuasive, despite the awkward objections. But many of those who were ready to accept evolution were critical of aspects of Darwin's particular account of how the process works. They were not committed to a literal interpretation of scripture, but many were troubled by the fact that natural selection theory seemed to leave no role for the guiding hand of divine providence: indeed, it seemed implicitly to deny the workings of providence altogether. Accordingly, a number of working biologists and liberal theologians attempted to formulate providential accounts of evolution: they wished to acknowledge that species have evolved, but wished also to show that God has had an active and creative hand in the process.

The American biologist, Asa Gray, pioneered this approach to Darwin's theory in some reviews that he wrote of *Origin of Species* in 1860. Darwin was sufficiently impressed by these reviews to have them published in Britain. Gray had readily acknowledged the explanatory power of Darwin's theory and had given it a sympathetic and knowledgeable exposition. But he rejected the idea that the process of evolution works by the natural selection of randomly occurring variations. Instead, he proposed 'that variation has been led along certain beneficial lines', by a providential power: the direction of evolution has been planned and guided.

In England, the Revd. Charles Kingsley took a similar line. After reading *Origin of Species*, he wrote to Darwin, in 1859,

> I have gradually learnt to see that it is just as noble a conception of Deity to believe that He created primal forms capable of self-development into all forms needful *pro tempore* and *pro loco* [at the appropriate times and places], as to believe that He required a fresh act of intervention to supply the *lacunaes* [gaps] which He himself had made. I question whether the former be not the loftier thought. (Quoted in F. Darwin, *The Life and Letters of Charles Darwin*, Vol. II, p.288)

These sorts of interpretations of evolution seemed to open the way to a speedy accommodation between Darwinism and liberal theology. Darwin was himself initially attracted to Gray's and Kingsley's interpretation. But the amiability of the exchanges in this area of the Darwinian debates – which contrasts sharply with the savagery of exchanges between outright objectors like the Bishop of Oxford and

Figure 7 The cartoon from Punch's Almanack *for 1882 pictures an evolutionary ascent from 'chaos', through worms, monkeys and pre-humans, on to a smart Victorian gentleman and, finally, to an old man. The old man is a caricature of the aged Darwin.*

Darwin's combative supporter, T. H. Huxley – concealed fundamental differences, and, as we shall see in a moment, Darwin eventually and decisively rejected the ideas that either variation or natural selection has been providentially guided.

Another source of objection to Darwin's theory was his account of the emergence of the human species. The *Origin of Species* clearly implied that humans have evolved, and in the *Descent of Man,* published in 1871, Darwin gave his full account of the evolution of humans from pre-humans. For a number of readers of Darwin's books, the human species was the sticking point. They were ready and willing to accept the evolution of plants and animals, and even Darwin's proposed evolutionary mechanism, but they were not ready to see humans and human society as the unplanned result of a process of accidental variation and natural selection. Those who were conventional Christians had automatic objections of the sort voiced by the Bishop of Oxford. Humans were supposed to have been made in the image of God; they have immortal souls; they have fallen from grace. What was to become of such concepts if humans have evolved, in imperceptible stages, from the brutes? But even if these Christian objections could somehow be surmounted, there was still the imaginative problem of responding to the prospect of an evolutionary ancestry for oneself. You had to be able to go to the zoo and gaze through the bars at a gorilla or a chimpanzee in the knowledge that you were closely related, and in the knowledge that the processes that have shaped them, have shaped you. This was no easy matter for Victorians, who had been brought up on the story of Adam and Eve, and who were morbidly sensitive about matters of decency, dignity and savagery. A complete acceptance of Darwin's theory required Victorians to undertake a major re-assessment of their image of themselves (see Figure 8).

Brought up, as we are now, on a diet, not of Adam and Eve, but of television wildlife programmes that simply assume complete evolutionary continuity between human and animal, we might be tempted to underestimate the psychological strain felt by those Victorians who took Darwin's theory seriously. The strain was sufficiently great for one of Darwin's greatest influences and most

A LOGICAL REFUTATION OF MR. DARWIN'S THEORY.

Jack (who has been reading passages from the "Descent of Man" to the Wife whom he adores, but loves to tease). "So you see, Mary, Baby is Descended from a Hairy Quadruped, with Pointed Ears and a Tail. We all are!"
Mary. "Speak for yourself, Jack! I'm not Descended from Anything of the Kind, I beg to say; and Baby takes after me. So, there!"

Figure 8 Cartoon from Punch, *April 1871.*

respected colleagues, the geologist Sir Charles Lyell, to jeopardize the coherence of his own theories: he was finally incapable of seeing himself as a product of evolution. Here is an entry from one of his private journals, journals in which he brooded obsessively on the problems of human evolution.

> It is somewhat irreverent to fear that any discovery will derogate from our conception of the dignity of the Creator. The real apprehension, however, if the truth be told, the sensitiveness, is founded on this: that the dignity of Man is at stake.
>
> It is the genealogy of Man which is rendered less imposing. And if it were lowered, if we were led to estimate less highly the position of Man in the Universe, no doubt it would be a loss — it would render our hopes less elevated. (Wilson (ed.), *Sir Charles Lyell's Scientific Journals on the Species Question*, p. 330)

This concern about the 'dignity of Man' prevented Lyell, one of the most eminent scientists, and a man of very liberal theological views, from ever fully accepting Darwin's theory.

What of Darwin himself? What were his own religious views, and what implications did he think his theory had for the notion that the world was designed by a good and wise god? You can try to answer these questions for yourself by looking at a couple of primary sources. One is an extract from his autobiography, and the other is a letter that he wrote to Asa Gray, the biologist who had attempted to supply a providential account of natural selection theory. Your reading will not settle the questions finally, for Darwin's views changed over the years and were never entirely consistent. In a sense, he never made up his mind. Also, bear in mind that neither the autobiography nor the letter was written with a view to publication. They are private documents. We are catching Darwin off his guard, not examining carefully prepared public statements.

Exercise

Now read extracts II.4 and II.9 of the Course Reader, with the following questions in mind.

1 What caused Darwin to lose faith in the truth of the Bible?

2 Did his scientific work have any bearing on his beliefs about whether or not the world has been designed by a good and wise God?

3 What views does he have about the reliability of human thought?

Discussion

It is plain that Darwin's loss of faith in the truth of the Bible had nothing to do with evolution. It had to do with what he saw as the incredibility of miracles, the unreliability of the testimony of the Gospels, and the immorality of eternal damnation. He says that disbelief slowly crept over him. In this respect, he was no different from those Victorian doubters who know nothing of biology — the sort of people discussed in sections 2 'The varieties of Victorian religion' and 4 'Challenges to orthodoxy from within the church'.

Darwin's views on the designfulness of nature, on the other hand, do seem to flow from his evolutionary work. He says that he has reached only 'vague conclusions', but these conclusions are that there is no more design exhibited in variation and natural selection than in 'the course which the wind blows'. His theory, he says, invalidates the notion that the world has been providentially designed. Too many features of the plant and animal world are morally repugnant. What sort of god would have designed insects whose offspring, developing within the bodies of caterpillars, eat their hosts alive, from the inside outward? Yet he finds it impossible to conceive of the universe as being the 'result of blind chance or necessity'. He never resolved the inconsistency, although he wrote, in a sentence added to the autobiography later, that his belief in the need to postulate a god as the originator of the universe had weakened.

Lastly, he doubts the trustworthiness of the human mind when it attempts to make statements about the origin of the universe. The subject, he says 'is too profound for the human intellect. A dog might as well speculate on the mind of Newton.' The animal origin of the human mind, and the effects of educational conditioning, he suggests, make it a dubious instrument for discovering ultimate truths. It is significant, and entirely typical of Darwin, that in the autobiography, when he is searching for an analogy for the human difficulty of throwing off belief in God, he finds it in the behaviour of monkeys, and their instinctive fear of snakes. The whole impetus of Darwin's theorizing about human behaviour was to seek rudimentary forms of that behaviour in animals.

If you have found these extracts from Darwin's private writings interesting, you might care to work through an extract from one of his mature, published books. In extract II.8 in the Course Reader you will find the concluding pages of his *Variation of Animals and Plants under Domestication* (1868). There, you can see him pondering, once again, some of the problems that his theory raised. The scientific theory of species origins, he is quite sure, is all-sufficient: there is no room left for God's hand. Yet is the notion that the universe has not been designed acceptable? Darwin writes in a low-key, diffident way, but he takes you to the heart of the major Victorian challenge to the Christian view of the world.

5.7 CONCLUSION

The most persistent symbol of the relationship between evolution and religion in Victorian Britain that has come down to us, is the angry public encounter between the Bishop of Oxford and T. H. Huxley at the 1860 meeting of the British Association for the Advancement of Science, at Oxford. The Bishop ridiculed those who believed that humans had brute ancestors, and, in reply, Huxley denounced the Bishop for his biological incompetence. Great events need symbols, but for an event as diffuse as the impact of Darwin's theory on Victorian consciousness, no symbol will be entirely adequate. It seems to me that the most profound and sensitive probings of the implications of evolution theory came from scientists themselves, imbued as they were with the Christianity in which they had been educated. Nonetheless, the public encounter at Oxford does stand for something important. The Bishop knew that a stand had to be made. He saw clearly that Darwin's theory was incompatible with any form of Christianity that he could recognize, and he manfully, if ultimately ignorantly, strode out to defend his religion.

6 RELIGION AND VICTORIAN PAINTING

As you work through this section you will need to refer to the *Illustration Booklet*.

When religion was so strong an influence on the lives of the Victorians, it would be surprising if it had not affected their art. Indeed, it affected not only their *making of* art but their *looking at* art too. The Victorians' experience of art was bound up with their expectations, beliefs and assumptions about their world. In this section, we shall be looking at a fairly wide range of images – from biblical scenes to landscapes – in order to examine how the relationship between art and religion was perceived. I want to ask a basic but important question:

1   What did a 'religious art' mean in the mid-Victorian context?

And then, given the crises and controversies you have been studying so far, I shall go on to ask:

2   How did works of art relate to debates within the established Church? and

3   How can Victorian paintings be seen in terms of contemporary beliefs and challenges to religious belief?

I shall concentrate on the years up to 1860 and the work of the Pre-Raphaelite group of artists, the critic Ruskin and the artist William Dyce. For in Victorian Britain – at least in its middle years – art was seen as inextricably linked with social, moral and religious matters. The view of art prevalent today – that art is independent from such matters as these – is a view that developed over the period you are studying. By the 1880s and 1890s, some artists (though by no means *all* artists) had found it more desirable to keep the religion – and the moralizing tone – out of their art.

6.1   PRE-RAPHAELITISM, RUSKIN AND RELIGIOUS ART

The Pre-Raphaelite Brotherhood was established in 1848 by three young painters: William Holman Hunt, Dante Gabriel Rossetti and John Everett Millais. Others later joined them, but it is these three who will concern us here. 'P.R.B.' was the initially secret monogram of this highly self-conscious group who had met as students at the Royal Academy Schools.

By looking at Pre-Raphaelite painting and religion, our view of their work will inevitably be weighted towards only one of its aspects – but an important aspect nevertheless. Although the Pre-Raphaelites were by no means exclusively painters of religious or biblical themes, one of the initial aims of the group was to revitalize religious art. Moreover, the art of the past which most interested the Pre-Raphaelites was the essentially religious imagery of the mediaeval period and the early Renaissance – that is, art which predated Raphael (1483–1520, see Colour plates 5, 6 and 7, discussed in Units 10–12 *Introduction to Art History*). Following the critic Ruskin, they thought that art had begun its decline with Raphael and the High Renaissance. Their views of the art of the past (sweeping and iconoclastic as indeed they often were) related to their evaluation of contemporary art: it was a reaction to what they saw as the degenerate, Raphaelesque tradition represented by the Royal Academy. Bear in mind that the Pre-Raphaelites' attitudes were not typical of Victorian artists generally, but their work and aspirations can tell us something about the norms and conventions of Victorian art which they adapted, modified or rejected.

Units 18–19 Religion: Conformity and Controversy

In the academic tradition, biblical subjects were considered a branch of history painting – the most highly esteemed genre. Let us think first about the way the Pre-Raphaelites' work related to that of their contemporaries and to the recent tradition of religious painting, in order to establish what was unusual, and what was conventional about their art.

Exercise

Please look carefully at three colour plates in the *Illustration Booklet*:

1   Sir Charles Eastlake *Christ Blessing Little Children* (1839, Colour plate 19). Sir Charles Eastlake became President of the Royal Academy in 1850. Though Colour plate 19 is an earlier work, it represents a type of painting that co-existed with that of Dyce and Millais in the mid-Victorian period.

2   William Dyce *Joash Shooting the Arrow of Deliverance* (1844, Colour plate 20). Dyce was a generation older than the Pre-Raphaelites, but he was sympathetic to their aims and introduced Ruskin to their work. He had been made a Royal Academician in 1844, the year this picture was highly praised at the annual Royal Academy Exhibition. It depicts a scene from the Old Testament Book of Kings: King Joash is advised by the Prophet Elisha to shoot an arrow in the direction of his enemy in order to free Israel from Syrian domination.

3   Millais *Christ in the Carpenter's Shop* (1849–50, Colour plate 21). Exhibited at the 1850 Royal Academy show. It depicts the kneeling Virgin next to the young Christ, with John the Baptist to the right and Joseph at work at his bench.

All these paintings depict religious subjects, but note down what differences are striking in the treatment of each.

Discussion

I would comment on the duller, shadowy tones of the Eastlake, compared with the precise and heightened description of the Dyce and the Millais. Eastlake's background is unspecific; Dyce has paid attention to the archaeological accuracy of his scene; Millais carefully locates the place, the workshop, with the minute, even obsessive treatment of the woodshavings on the floor. Eastlake's figure types are more sentimental and idealized than those painted by Dyce or Millais. Eastlake represented the Raphaelesque as it had degenerated into sweetness rather than substance, trite in its 'ideal' types and its fondness for chiaroscuro and mellowed tones. The Pre-Raphaelites objected to the use of dark, sombre colours in academic painting which, when combined with a loose handling of paint, they called 'slosh' – a tradition they saw as typified by the work of the eighteenth-century artist Sir Joshua ('Sloshua') Reynolds, first President of the Royal Academy (see Plate 22).

The Pre-Raphaelites derived a great deal, on the other hand, from Dyce, who had long been interested in the Italian 'primitives' (i.e. artists before Raphael). The Pre-Raphaelites were indebted, for their artistic technique, to Dyce and others who had heightened their palette by painting on a white, rather than a toned, ground (with the effect of brightening rather than mellowing the colours applied on the surface prepared in this way). With this technique, they emulated the luminosity and brilliance of colour they found in the work of the 'primitives'.

Remember, however, that both Dyce and Millais were trained in the classical tradition and depended on illusionistic devices and technical skills thus learnt – they did not 'unlearn' their academic training but incorporated references to earlier art and archaic conventions. In order to be seen as 'primitive', Millais' picture presupposed a knowledge of those conventions; and as a large-scale religious subject, it represented an ambitious bid for success in the established forum of the Royal Academy. The question of the Victorian interest in the 'primitives' is discussed in Television programme 21 *Victorian Views of the Art of the Past*.

Ruskin saw the Raphaelesque as synonymous with the degeneracy of high art, prised apart from its true religious purpose: 'In early times *art was employed for the display of religious facts*; now, *religious facts were employed for the display of art.*' (Ruskin, *Modern Painters*, Vol. 3, p.55)

For Ruskin, Raphael's cartoon for the *Charge to St Peter* (Plate 39), demonstrated only an apparent, and basically deceitful, fidelity to nature; what is more, it merely served the cause of the Vatican and the papal heresy of Petrine Supremacy. Thus with the greater complexity of the artist's knowledge of art, of perspective and chiaroscuro, for example, true religious content was sacrificed for the sensual display of clever technical skill. In Ruskin's terms, the work of Fra Angelico (see Colour plate 23) was not entirely accurate but it was redolent of the artist's feeling for his subject. Ruskin used the models of mediaeval and early Renaissance artists as a means to criticize the art of his own time – and, more broadly, its faithlessness and false values. He believed that art was expressive of the period in which it was produced. As opposed to the honesty and innocence expressed in the art of earlier times, contemporary art was in general insincere and affected, expressing the values of a degenerate society. He thus made an exception of those artists whom he felt aspired to truth, even though the Pre-Raphaelites 'in no wise represent the modern school' (*Modern Painters*, Vol. 3, p.278).

Look now at the reproduction of Rossetti's *Ecce Ancilla Domini!* ('Behold the Handmaiden of the Lord!', 1849–50, Colour plate 22). It is a picture of the Annunciation, where Mary learns her destiny from the Angel Gabriel. This was a common subject in the repertoire of fifteenth-century Italian artists such as Fra Angelico (Colour plate 23), so admired by the Pre-Raphaelites. The painting contains the traditional symbols of the Annunciation; for example, the lily is symbolic of the Virgin's purity and the dove of the Holy Ghost. It does not follow, however, that through the use of similar motifs the works share the same meaning. For the adoption of such a symbolic system in the mid-nineteenth century was deliberately archaic. Thus the Rossetti was not just a representation of the Annunciation, but a representation of a fifteenth-century tradition of Annunciation paintings. Rossetti painted the Virgin from a living model (see drawing, Plate 41) in an attempt to avoid the kind of ideal type you saw in the Eastlake, but also gives her a flat, gold halo. This marks an 'updating' and re-interpretation of tradition as well as self-conscious reference to it.

Another reason why a Pre-Raphaelite religious image does not mean the same as its fifteenth-century model is to be found in the difference of function. For the art of the fifteenth century had a specific religious and devotional function that was either public or private (as Erika Langmuir discussed in Units 10–12 *Introduction to Art History*). Religious art was seen as an aid to devotion: the setting for an altarpiece was, for instance, the altar of a chapel or church at which mass was said. Pre-Raphaelite painting, on the other hand, was produced in very different social and historical circumstances. Unlike Fra Angelico's picture, Rossetti's was not produced as a response to a particular commission, but for sale on the open market. Millais' *Christ in the Carpenter's Shop* (Colour plate 21) was intended for the annual Royal Academy exhibition. This was the major forum for showing works of art in a *secular* setting. The picture was sold (in fact on the morning before it was submitted to the Royal Academy exhibition) to the picture dealer Henry Farrer and later sold to Thomas Plint, a Leeds stockbroker and Christian Socialist. Of course a picture does not have to be painted for a church to carry religious meaning; what I'm suggesting is that pictures are interpreted in a context and that by and large, the Victorian context was secular.

I say 'by and large' because during the period painters also worked to commission – for instance, in the decoration of churches. What is more, the decoration of churches was the subject of much debate and controversy. The Protestant Church traditionally distrusted the ritualistic and 'sensual' use of art in religious ceremony which was associated with Romanism. However, there was a tradition of including paintings in decoration – particularly in High Anglican churches. As you know, the Oxford Movement had a strong interest in ceremonial and ritual practices, familiar to Catholics but not to Anglicans. In Television programme 18 *The Victorian High Church*, Colin Cunningham looks at two High Anglican London churches and the ways in which architecture and decoration were designed to serve ceremonial needs. As you will see in the programme, decoration meant a whole decorative scheme, including church furnishings and stained glass. (See Plate 44 for William Dyce's study for a fresco, All Saints, Margaret St.) Of the initial group of the Pre-Raphaelites, it was Rossetti who became most involved in church decoration. He produced an altarpiece *The Seed of David* (Plate 43, 1858–64) for Llandaff Cathedral and worked with the firm of 'Fine Art Workmen in painting, carving and the metals', started by William Morris in 1861. This firm, discussed in detail in Units 31–32, was responsible for the decoration of many churches, including St Martin-on-the-Hill, Scarborough (see Figures 9 and 10).

Figure 9 Pulpit, St Martin-on-the-Hill, Scarborough. The eight front panels were painted by Campfield to designs by Ford Madox Brown and William Morris. Brown designed the four Evangelists above (Matthew, Mark, Luke and John). Morris designed the four Doctors of the Church below (Ambrose, Gregory, Jerome and Augustine), figures from the Catholic tradition which show the influence of the Oxford Movement. On the side of the pulpit Rossetti depicted the Annunciation. (Photo: P. H. K. Smith)

In both their decorative schemes and their paintings with a religious subject-matter, the Pre-Raphaelites' references to earlier traditions are, as I have said,

6 Religion and Victorian painting

Figure 10 Edward Burne-Jones, Cartoon for the Annunciation, *1862, Birmingham City Art Gallery. Adapted to a circular format, this design was used for the stained glass of the Western Rose window at St Martin-on-the-Hill, Scarborough. Notice the lily, traditional symbol of purity. St Martin's was an early commission for Morris's firm, which played a central role in the revival of the art of stained glass in the Victorian period. Another example is Middleton Cheney, Northants, 1864, see Plate 119 in the* Illustration Booklet.

deliberately archaic. Let us now ask how those references related to contemporary interests and beliefs. Look again at Millais' *Christ in the Carpenter's Shop*, where the symbolism depends heavily on the traditions and conventions of past art. For instance, 'pre-figurative' symbolism is used: the bowl of water carried by John looks forward to the baptism of Christ and the drop of blood on Christ's foot prefigures the sacrifice of the Crucifixion. This kind of symbolism can be related to contemporary forms of religious belief and practice. It depends on a contemporary preoccupation with reading the scriptures in terms of 'prefigurative' types and symbols and an accompanying acceptance of a pre-ordained, divine plan. This was a standard preoccupation of sermon writers. This device was central to the work of Holman Hunt. In *The Finding of the Saviour in the Temple* (1854–5, 1856–60, Plate 40) an inscription in Latin and Hebrew on the golden gate bears an Old Testament prophecy from Malachi 31: 'and the Lord, whom ye seek, shall suddenly come to his temple'. And in *The Shadow of Death* (1870–3, Plate 42) Christ is shown in the carpenter's shop in a position that prefigures the Crucifixion.

Exercise

In the light of your study of *Essays and Reviews*, what comment would you make on this use of pre-figurative symbolism?

Units 18–19 Religion: Conformity and Controversy

Discussion

It may seem that by 1860, and during the earlier years of religious controversy, this use of pre-figurative symbolism was rather old-fashioned in relation to the new thinking within the Church. Indeed, when the controversy was at its height, Hunt continued to use the device. What was 'up-to-date' in theology, then, was not necessarily so in art.

The preference for such symbolism developed in an attempt to revitalize religious art through reference to older artistic traditions. One of the main motives was to retrieve the simplicity and purity of earlier art: that is, to lay stress on faith rather than sophistry. Furthermore, in Hunt's work, predictive symbolism was not simply *opposed* to historical accuracy. Indeed, Hunt visited the Holy Land (1854–6) in order that his settings and figure types should be scrupulously observed. So there is a complex relationship, but no symmetry, between art and religion.

6.2 ART AND RELIGIOUS CONTROVERSY

This exercise leads us to look in more detail at art in relation to debates within the church. It may be hard to imagine what could be so controversial about Millais' *Christ in the Carpenter's Shop* – a seemingly innocuous biblical scene. But the picture was fiercely attacked by critics when it was exhibited in 1850. On one level, this reaction can be better understood if the work is matched against normal expectations of what was fitting and appropriate – at one extreme, the sentimental and conventional Eastlake. Many reviewers objected to the banality and distortion of the figures, depicted with all their imperfections: these types were seen as inappropriate vehicles for religious sentiment. Dickens, for instance, wrote of the kneeling Virgin: 'she would stand out from the rest of the company as a monster in the vilest cabaret in France or in the lowest gin-shop in England' (*Household Words*, 13 June 1850). But these objections were not merely artistic – they were interlocked with contemporary religious controversy – particularly the intense anti-Catholicism of 1850–51. To contemporaries, the picture smacked of Romanism.

According to Holman Hunt, Millais' *Christ in the Carpenter's Shop* was prompted by a sermon given, during 1849, by a member of the Oxford Movement. Indeed, the picture can be seen to relate to contemporary controversies in that it incorporates Tractarian and Ecclesiologist ideas. Millais had deliberately constructed a complicated symbolic scheme to which each element of the picture contributes – a scheme that was decidedly High Church in emphasis. It is likely that such references would have been recognized by a public familiar with current debates. In this context, the bench not only refers symbolically to the altar but suggests a High Church emphasis on the sacrament of the communion and the recurring mass; and that not only is the baptism of Christ prefigured in the bowl of water carried by John, but this feature also relates to the Tractarian emphasis on child baptism and regeneration through baptism. Indeed the Low Church Ruskin was never happy with the picture. And in his defence of Pre-Raphaelitism in a letter to *The Times* in 1851, he stressed his reservations about the Tractarian aspects of their work (Course Reader, extract IV.1).

The exact nature of the Pre-Raphaelites' relationship with the High Church movement is problematic. Millais' involvement ceased as abruptly as it had begun. Rossetti's position is ambivalent, although his family was High Anglican. Holman Hunt was the most committed, consistent and practising Christian with a missionary zeal. But even his position is not entirely straightforward, for he was associated with the High Church movement but had Evangelical leanings, for example, in his preoccupation with conversion. His *The Light of the World* (Colour plate 17) was shown at the Royal Academy in 1854, with this quotation inscribed on the frame: 'Behold I stand at the door, and knock: if any man hear my voice, and open the door, I will come into him, and will stop with him, and he with me.' (Revelations 3.20)

This painting was enormously popular and widely reproduced. It was bought by Thomas Coombes, who was deeply involved in the High Church movement. But it was also rated extremely highly by the Low Church Ruskin, who saw it as 'one of the very noblest works of sacred art ever produced in this or any other age' (letter to *The Times*, 5 May 1854). He defended it against critics who objected to the 'common', naturalistic elements unsuited to a spiritual scene. Holman Hunt had worked on the background outside, at night, in order to render the moonlit scene in what he saw as the most faithful way possible, and Ruskin felt Christ was thus depicted as a 'living presence'. Although many Pre-Raphaelite paintings were accused of Romanism, they clearly worked on many more levels than mere propaganda for a given position. (*The Light of the World* is discussed further in Colin Cunningham's 'Reproduction and dissemination of visual images' in Unit 22.)

Up till now, we have been discussing a 'religious art' that is defined by its obviously religious subject-matter — stories from the Bible, for instance. But for art to carry a religious meaning in the mid-Victorian period, it did not have to have an overtly religious subject. For example, Holman Hunt exhibited *The Hireling Shepherd* at the Royal Academy in 1852 (Colour plate 35). This picture will be discussed at greater length in the discussion of that exhibition in Unit 22. But note here that it was later explained by Hunt as a critique of the contemporary clergy's neglect of its flock. This is an ostensibly *secular* scene, then, with an underlying commentary on the divisive nature of schisms within the Church: the shepherd does not minister to his flock but dallies with the shepherdess. This symbolism was further veiled in Hunt's later *Our English Coasts, 1852 (Strayed Sheep)* (1852, Colour plate 25); here sheep have been allowed to stray to the cliff-top through the implied neglect of the absent shepherd. Whilst working on *The Hireling Shepherd*, Hunt read Ruskin's *Notes on the construction of sheepfolds* (1851). Here Ruskin wrote '... the schism between the so-called Evangelical and High Church Parties in Britain, is enough to shake men's faith in the truth or existence of Religion at all ...'. A concern for the danger of disunity, then, could be shared by the Low Church and Evangelical Ruskin and by Hunt with his sympathies for the High Church movement. Also shared was the symbolic language of 'Christ's sheep' and the 'sheepfold' as the Church. A certain type of religious language, then, was a pre-requisite for the conception of the work.

6.3 PAINTING, BELIEF AND SCIENCE

> ... sacred art, so far from being exhausted, has yet to attain the development of its highest branches; and the task, or privilege, yet remains for mankind, to produce an art which shall be at once entirely skilful and entirely *sincere* ... (Ruskin, *Modern Painters*, Vol. III, pp.62–3)

So wrote Ruskin in 1856. This was a few years before *Essays and Reviews* and Darwin's *Origin of Species* were published, but nonetheless it was written at a time when religious belief and orthodoxy were under critical attack. It may seem odd, then, that in a period of religious doubt and controversy, the most influential art critic of the day could argue that the greatest religious art was yet to be produced. Ruskin was greatly distressed by the divisiveness of contemporary religious conflict, but he was optimistic about science. For Ruskin, the work of scientists could increase knowledge of the world, and thus an understanding of 'God's work'. In this respect, he stood in the intellectual tradition that Darwin was to demolish (see pp. 43–4). The first volume of *Modern Painters* was published in 1843 and was concerned with Turner and the art of landscape painting. Ruskin believed that Turner and the Pre-Raphaelites had laid the foundations for this great period of sacred art. He was not simply referring here to paintings of religious subjects. Indeed, Hunt's use of the landscape motif in *Strayed Sheep* shows his dependence on Ruskin's idea of 'nature-scripture', where nature exemplified the divine. That 'Nature' in all its geological and botanical complexity could be expressive of a divine Truth was not seen as contradictory; instead, Ruskin's view of art assumed its connectedness with science, nature and all aspects of human knowledge.

The findings of geologists had obliged those Victorians who were not slavishly committed to a belief in the literal truth of every word in the Bible to reckon the age of the earth in many millions, rather than a few thousand years. Moreover, the geological record of these millions of years was a record of the extinction of countless species of plants and animals. In Tennyson's words, Nature seemed to be saying:

> ... a thousand types are gone;
> I care for nothing, all shall go.

William Dyce's painting, *Pegwell Bay: A Recollection of October 5th, 1858* (1860, Colour plate 27) can be considered, like Tennyson's poem *In Memoriam*, a manifestation of the Victorians' reconsideration of their place within the new and desolate timescale of the earth's history.

Such a claim, you may object, is a bit far fetched. After all, isn't *Pegwell Bay* merely a depiction of Victorians at the seaside – in the same vein as Frith's hugely successful *Ramsgate Sands* (1854, Colour plate 26)? In my view, the answer to that is both yes and no. Both pictures do represent the beach as a site of Victorian leisure – albeit, in the Dyce, the rather earnest leisure pursuit of shell and fossil collecting. But the pictures manifest very different interests. Whereas Frith depicted individuals from various social strata at a seaside *resort*, Dyce emphasized those aspects of the nearby Pegwell Bay that were most resistant to colonization by the urban middle classes.

Compare Dyce's watercolour sketch of 1857 (Plate 45) with the completed *Pegwell Bay* (Colour plate 27). The artist has made several alterations; he has included more figures – an artist carrying his materials on the far right, and members of the painter's family collecting shells on the beach. The cliffs are treated with scrupulous attention to the details of their geological strata and incrustation of fossils. Donati's comet (first observed on 2 June 1858) is depicted in the sky above the two central foreground figures. Although it is difficult to see in reproduction, I assure you that it is there. The comet was at its brightest on 5 October, the date specified in Dyce's title. It has thus been suggested that this painting relates to Tennyson's 'terrible muses' – geology, on the one hand, and astronomy, on the other (Pointon, 'The representation of time in painting...'). Human life, then, was seen as dwarfed by the dimensions of time and space. Dyce, like Ruskin, was interested in geology, and was familiar with the ideas of geologists like Charles Lyell. Neither saw the geological evidence of the earth's history as irreconcilable with Christian belief. *Pegwell Bay* was exhibited at the 1860 Academy Exhibition; so too was his *Man of Sorrows* (Plate 46), depicting Christ in the wilderness. Again, close attention is paid to the details of the rocky highland landscape in which Christ sits – indicating the compatibility, rather than conflict, of Faith with geological history. Both these pictures were praised by the critic of the *Atheneum*, 'Journal of Literature, Science and the Fine Arts'. But he did criticize Dyce for his lack of realism in *Man of Sorrows*, saying that he should have set his scene in an Eastern landscape. This demand for historical accuracy was partly due to the precedent of artists who had travelled to the Holy Land to observe the 'actual' context of the biblical stories; Holman Hunt is an example.

To sum up, let me reiterate some of the main points of this discussion:

1 Pictures with biblical subjects were considered a branch of 'History Painting' and mostly produced, like other types of painting, for sale to individual collectors. The wider dissemination of religious images was achieved through engravings – to be discussed in Unit 22.

2 The Pre-Raphaelite treatment of biblical subjects was closely related to Victorian debates within the Church and to the High Church Movement.

3 Religious significance was not confined to pictures with a biblical subject. A broad range of works dealt indirectly with belief and crises in belief.

Ruskin wrote of the difficulties of being a good art critic, who, given the richness of art, needed to be informed of the widest spectrum of human knowledge. He envisaged a unity of art, science and religion. As we shall see in Units 31–32, by the end of the period, views about the kind of knowledge that went into the making of art, and about what could be learnt from art, had become far narrower. In the 1880s and 1890s, art itself could be seen to have taken on some of the guise of a religious cult – in the new aesthetics of 'art for art's sake'.

7 RELIGION IN THE POETRY OF TENNYSON AND HOPKINS

In Memoriam A.H.H. Obiit MDCCCXXXIII was published anonymously on 1 June 1850, exactly half way through the nineteenth century. Its success was instantaneous and extraordinary: 60,000 copies were sold in a few months. It averaged one new 'edition' (reprinting) per year for the next twenty years and it remained so popular that there were several 'editions' in the 1880s. Its title means 'In Memory of A.H.H. who died in 1833'. Its form has occasioned much puzzlement and debate. It is probably best viewed as rather similar to Shakespeare's famous series of sonnets – as a sequence of individual poems relating to a common 'story'. Though the poems – 131 of them, plus Prologue and Epilogue – are not, like sonnets, equal in size, all their stanzas rhyme *abba*, and their lines are all in a common English metre, the 'iambic tetrameter'. The 'story' covers about three years, marked by three Christmasses. It begins with a funeral and ends with a marriage, and the 'speaker' of the sequence moves from grief and religious doubt, occasioned by the death of a dear friend, to greater poise and towards emotional, if not intellectual, certainty.

As you have gathered already, it can be regarded as the quintessential 'Victorian' work of literature. It consoled the Queen herself after the death of Albert – 'Next to the Bible', she told its author, '"In Memoriam" is my comfort.' Its vast sales, though, meant that it brought pleasure and reassurance to readers of much lower status. On its author's eighty-third birthday, in 1892, an artisan from Newcastle wrote to him:

> ...Your poetry has been such a goodly gift to me... Sometimes horrid doubt throws its darkening veil about me, there is so much in this life formless and void of cheer, your verse sets my feet aright. 'In Memoriam' has brought me better faith, clearer mental vision, higher ultimate hope. (Charles Tennyson, *Alfred Tennyson*, p.529)

It is easy to understand why the poem was so loved. It speaks about bereavement and grief, common experiences, in a reassuringly 'traditional' way – the metre is familiar, the diction noble. Thought and feeling are usually (though not quite always) very clear, and ideas are largely communicated through imagery which vividly evokes English life and landscape.

Exercise

Read carefully the famous poem, No. 7 in the sequence, printed below. Try to define in a few phrases how the speaker perceives the external reality which he evokes, and see if you can spot 'technical' devices by which the poem creates emotional effects.

Units 18–19 Religion: Conformity and Controversy

> Dark house, by which once more I stand
>   Here in the long unlovely street,
>   Doors, where my heart was used to beat
> So quickly, waiting for a hand,
>
> A hand that can be clasp'd no more –
>   Behold me, for I cannot sleep,
>   And like a guilty thing I creep,
> At earliest morning to the door.
>
> He is not here; but far away
>   The noise of life begins again,
>   And ghastly thro' the drizzling rain
> On the bald street breaks the blank day.

Discussion

I would say that apart from the 'drizzling rain', the adjectives all evoke 'feeling' not 'fact'. 'Unlovely' applied to a street means 'I don't like it, at the moment'. 'Bald' vaguely suggests rather boring architecture, but is no more descriptive than 'blank' applied to 'day'. The overall patterning of *sound* is very striking and important. Did you notice how the same vowel – long 'a' – ends every line in the third stanza, its flat sound reinforcing the sense of despair evoked by 'ghastly', 'bald', 'blank'? Despair is complicated (as grief often is) by feelings of unworthiness – 'like a guilty thing'.

This author is a highly skilled constructor of feelings in verse. He is not spontaneously 'reporting'. The feeling in 'Dark House' is easy for us to relate to because it isn't closely tied to any one 'real' street. And *In Memoriam* as a whole has to be read not as a biographical record but as an attempt to 'universalize' private grief.

Exercise

Please now read section 98 of *In Memoriam* in the Course Reader, extract II.11, and try to relate it to what's just been said.

Discussion

This comes quite late in the whole sequence, and represents a very different mood. It isn't famous in its own right, like 'Dark House', as an anthology piece, but it has an important place in the overall effect of *In Memoriam*. Here the speaker, addressing a friend who is about to visit Vienna, where A.H.H. died, explicitly recognizes that there may be a gap between his own subjective feelings (which associated Vienna with evil) and objective reality, such as his own dead friend (stanzas 6–8) evoked for him. The rocket is one imagined by the speaker, but imagined as existing in its own right, outside his feelings. His dead friend's words, remembered, point him back towards living realities. When people are depressed or grieving, their friends will try to persuade them that 'life goes on', and encourage them to take an interest in the life outside themselves. Section 98 shows such interest emerging. The power of *In Memoriam* to move and reassure its readers – its *authority* as a religious testament – stemmed in great part from its 'common sense' view of the processes of feeling involved in deep grief, then firm recovery. Its author would strike Queen Victoria, or a Newcastle artisan, as someone who 'understood people', had his 'feet on the ground'.

He was also a brilliant popularizer of up-to-date ideas about the universe. To be precise, he clearly knew of

1   The *Mécanique Celeste* (1799–1825) by the Frenchman **Laplace** who had produced the 'nebular hypothesis' – that the solar system had been formed from an original gaseous nebula, which had produced a burning, but dying, sun and the cooler planets, including earth, which revolved round it. This theory carried with it the frightening suggestion that life on earth would eventually be extinguished.

2   Charles Lyell's *Principles of Geology* (1830–3) which tried to show that the face of the earth is entirely shaped by natural forces. Continents and islands, mountains, deserts, ice-caps, are all the result of erosion, sedimentation, climate and volcanic action, forces which over immense periods of time perpetually transform landscapes. Fossils visible in rocks (as at Pegwell Bay, depicted by Dyce) are the records of species which died out because they could not adapt to changing conditions. Despite the apparently 'materialistic' drive in his work, Lyell believed that his researches gave 'clear proofs of a Creative Intelligence, and of His foresight, wisdom and power'. But this did not really dispel the implications – disturbing for Wordsworthian Romantics as well as for biblical literalists – of his assertion that 'species cannot be immortal, but must perish one after the other, like the individuals which compose them'. Was man just a passing phenomenon, due to 'perish' at the hands of ruthless nature?

3   However, *Vestiges of the Natural History of Creation*, published anonymously in 1844 (it was by Robert Chambers) went cheerfully back to the formation of the solar system and traced the development of life up to its present highest form – the 'adult Caucasian' (i.e. 'white, European') human being. Many people disliked Chambers' implication, years before Darwin's *Origin of Species*, that man was part of the 'animal scale'. But the author of *In Memoriam* relished the idea that through all catastrophes and injustices mankind as a whole was evolving towards a higher level of being.

Because *In Memoriam* anticipated, in unexceptionably earnest and noble lines, some of the terms of the debate over Darwin, it didn't become 'out of date' after 1859: it still had power to reconcile the claims of science and religion and to reassure people that the former, with its enticing offer of material progress, needn't destroy faith in God and immortality.

Exercise

Please now read, or re-read, in the Course Reader, sections 21, 31, 35, 50, 53, 54, 55, 56, 95, 118, 120, 123, 124, and the Epilogue. Read as fast as you can, noticing allusions to current scientific ideas, and trends in thought.

Discussion

Section 21   This poem – you may feel it's a bit 'twee' – sets up a contrast between 'private sorrow', which the speaker claims he must express, and the public world, including Science, given a portentous capital. ('The latest moon' may refer, rather inexactly, to the discovery of the planet Neptune in 1846.)

Section 31   Here the speaker obliquely confronts the problem of the historicity of the Bible which, as you've learnt, would later exercise contributors to *Essays and Reviews*. St John's Gospel tells us that Lazarus rose from the grave. But alas, it does not report any description by Lazarus of his experiences as a dead man. The last two lines insinuate the grim thought that maybe John gathered that, according to Lazarus, there was no heaven or hell, nor afterlife.

Section 35   This poem explores that nasty possibility further. The third stanza draws on Lyell's ideas. Streams erode hills, the sediment creates new continents. But if materialists are right, if man is mere matter and death prevails – how can Love exist? Without hope of immortality, Love would be no more than 'mere fellowship' or – much worse – mere sexual gratification. The poem implicitly – and very cunningly – appeals to 'common sense'. The very existence of the higher emotion of Love so strongly felt by the speaker seems to contradict materialism.

Section 50   Likewise, this poem assumes that A.H.H., who is addressed, is immortal. That implicitly contradicts the horrid idea that men die out like flies – which is made to seem the product of a morbid nervous condition, itself susceptible of scientific explanation. Do you see how the poem works on a 'heads I win, tails you lose' basis as it moves towards its final assertion of faith in immortality?

Section 53 The loading of the argument here is clear. It is 'morally impossible', common sense insists, to believe that sowing one's wild oats, acting godlessly in youth, is somehow necessary. After all, A.H.H. was only 22 when *he* died, too young to have expiated such sins as he hadn't, in fact, committed. 'Philosophy', a term which then implicitly included 'Science', has its place, but taken beyond its 'mark' it might lead us to damnation.

Section 54 This famous poem ends pessimistically – we are in the darkest part of the sequence. Yet 'common sense' which the speaker shares with 'us' – '*we* trust' – contradicts the morbid thoughts of 'I' – 'what am I?'

Section 55 Here thoughts, including something rather like 'natural selection', are drawn from Tennyson's scientific reading. This poem reverses the tactics of its predecessor, with the key words 'feel' and 'hope' suggesting, at last, the speaker's will to believe, and the root of belief in devout 'feelings'.

Section 56 Nevertheless, worse implications still are found in Lyell. It's not that species – 'types' – survive while 'single' lives are discarded. The evidence of fossils – embedded in 'scarped cliff and quarried stone' – shows us that whole *species* have died out, like the dinosaurs, 'Dragons of the prime'. Man may follow them. In this poem, the burden of reassurance is carried by the word 'veil'. There are limits to human knowledge, that word insinuates, beyond which we – and scientists – can't see.

Section 95 This poem describes a moment of vision, or 'trance', which preludes and supports the optimism of the latter part of the sequence. Nature here is not 'red in tooth and claw' but charming and unfrightening, like the ermine moths evoked in stanza three (by the way, they seem to be the subject, not object of the verb 'lit' – 'alighted'). She is maternally protective – her trees lay 'dark arms about the field'. The words of the dead A.H.H. himself give reassurance to 'faith'. In editions down to the late 1870s,

> *His* living soul was flash'd on mine
> And Mine in *his* was wound...

which indicates a sense of mystic communion with the lost friend. The revised version is more impersonal, and suggests that the soul of the whole universe winds round the speaker. In both versions 'deep pulsations of the world' implies that the earth is suffused with divine personality, and 'Aeonian music', 'the music of the eons', evokes harmony as the governing principle of nature; the blows of death are part of a beautiful overall pattern. The reader might want more information about this remarkable spiritual event, this trance – but 'heads I win, tails you lose'. Speech is just a product of *matter*, and cannot describe the immaterial. However, the breeze can talk, and says 'the dawn, the dawn', at which point – with marvellous imagery – time is abolished, dawn and dusk unite in 'boundless day'.

Section 118 Chambers supplies inspiration. Evolution towards a higher 'type' is in progress, but man does not have to wait on the slow processes of nature. Just as he can take crude ore and make it into something useful (Victorian industrialization is here invoked in support of faith), so he can actively improve himself away from the lower animals, ape and tiger, still part of his nature.

Section 120 'Wiser man' is ironic. The speaker jeers at the pretensions of materialistic science.

Section 123 Though he still accepts Lyell's geological theories, they are countervailed by his 'dream' of his friend's immortality confirmed for him by the 'trance' of 95.

Section 124 Compare this poem with 54. The 'infant' of that is a 'child' in this, who has grown up enough to know that his father, God, is always near. And the *feeling* of 95 is an indestructible basis for faith. 'I have *felt.*'

Epilogue A marriage between an admired friend and the speaker's sister. This will produce a child – 'a soul shall draw from out the vast' – who will, in embryo, still represent lower phases in Chambers' 'animal scale', but will be closer than his parents to the 'crowning race' of perfect men. These will have perfect knowledge of nature, perfect science. And the dead A.H.H., born before his time, represented their perfection.

You may find this conclusion embarrassing — straightforward faith in inevitable human progress is now, at a guess, rare, and the author of *In Memoriam*, before he died, was no longer sure things were moving in the right direction. In 'Locksley Hall Sixty Years After' (1886) he wrote of:

> Evolution ever climbing after some ideal good,
> And Reversion ever dragging Evolution in the mud.

But for its early readers, the authority of the speaker's last words would have been reinforced by his 'common sense', his 'realism' — remember section 98 — and by his skilful deployment of images of family harmony. The central role of the family in human society and human happiness was very strongly felt, as the popular novels of the day show us. Christmas and New Year — the midwinter family festival — is built into the structure of *In Memoriam*. You might now read sections 28, 30 and 106. Family harmony, and the music of bells, evoke divinely inspired cosmic harmony. A marriage ceremony gives promise of the perpetuation of such rites, such harmony.

Harmony, of course, is suggested by the very skill by which *In Memoriam* arranges words in compelling, beautiful patterns. A friend of the author, Edward Fitzgerald (famous for his translation of Omar Khayyam), complained that *In Memoriam* is 'monstrous, and has that air of being evolved by a Poetical Machine of the highest order'. Thanks to a vast range of subject-matter, and subtle variation in the handling of its stanza, *In Memoriam* is not monotonous — it is hypnotic. A recent critic remarks that the sequence 'does not much claim — in argument, as distinct from mood and feelings — to be going forward but rather is turning round'. The stanza itself, he adds — rhyming *abba* — is especially suited to turning round rather than going forward (Ricks, *Tennyson*, pp.222, 224). The sequence circles round the initial experience of grief, always accepting as axiomatic the supreme goodness and intelligence of the dead A.H.H. before it finally reveals that he is, in effect, a type of Christ, of 'the Christ that is to be' in all men. The anguish and pessimism evoked in powerful sections are always held in rein by the solid, revolving, meditative stanza form, and the idealized, perfect hero.

The 'author of *In Memoriam*' was of course Alfred Tennyson. We think of him as 'Alfred *Lord* Tennyson', but he wasn't made a peer till thirty-three years after the publication of *In Memoriam*, and we completely misunderstand him and his role in Victorian England if we imagine him to be a stately, pompous pillar of the Establishment. He was extremely eccentric — a heavy drinker who chain-smoked a pipe, dressed in broadbrimmed hat and an odd Spanish cape which concealed habitually filthy linen, and took clumsy 'rustic' manners to the point of frequent rudeness, both intentional and inadvertent. His life till 1850 had been very unhappy. He was very short-sighted, and often ill. His father, a country parson in Lincolnshire, was an epileptic and alcoholic, whose temper got so bad that his children feared for their lives. Alfred's elder brother Charles, also a gifted poet, was for long periods addicted to opium, and of his younger brothers one succumbed for a time to alcoholism, another spent his whole adult life in a madhouse, and a third ('I am Septimus, the most morbid of the Tennysons') also sojourned awhile in a mental asylum in the course of a futile existence.

Yet at Cambridge University, Alfred had been befriended by a being who seemed god-like not only to the young poet, but also to another close friend, the future Prime Minister William Ewart Gladstone. Arthur Henry Hallam, son of a celebrated historian, had been a child prodigy, and seemed possessed of every talent needed for success in scholarship, literature or politics. He took to the eccentric Tennysons sufficiently well to become engaged to Alfred's sister Emily, so the great grief when he died suddenly wasn't the poet's alone in his family circle.

Figure 11 Alfred Lord Tennyson, photo by Cundall, 1861. (Source: Mansell Collection)

For seventeen years after Hallam died, Alfred, while gaining a modest reputation as a poet, lived a completely unsettled life. He was obsessed with his unfortunate heredity. Epilepsy, which he believed he might have from his father, was especially shameful as it was supposed to be the concomitant of masturbation; Alfred's sexual prudishness had its root in terrible fears. He believed himself poor, though he was never in want, and that was another reason for not marrying, besides the 'black blood' of the Tennysons which he imagined he might pass on to his sons. Only after he became sure, in his mid thirties, that his deep depressions were not the product of epilepsy or incipient madness was he able to contemplate marriage seriously. It is easy to see why memories of his happy friendship with Hallam obsessed him, and why, over seventeen years, he wrote (in a dirty butcher's account book) the 'elegies' which became *In Memoriam*.

It is clear that he must have *felt* the problems of faith with especial acuteness. Luckily he had reacted against the Calvinism of his Aunt Mary, who believed herself to be saved and him damned. ('Alfred, Alfred, whenever I look at you I think of the words, Depart from me, ye cursed, into everlasting fire.') He didn't believe in Hell. And he did have enough intelligence to cope with the new scientific ideas, about which he was very curious, so that they didn't hurl him into madness.

At the age of 41, his life was suddenly transformed. *In Memoriam* made him famous (its authorship was soon known). Two weeks after its publication he married at last. Wordsworth, the Poet Laureate, had just died; Prince Albert liked

Tennyson's work and he got the post. Next year, Millais, the Pre-Raphaelite, exhibited at the Royal Academy a painting based on the new Laureate's poem 'Mariana'. For the rest of his long life (he died in 1892) one of Tennyson's greater problems was that of coping with fame comparable to that of a modern pop star. Money ceased to be a problem. As 'the People's Poet', he was earning unprecedented sums. By 1871, a New York journal offered him £1,000 for a single poem – *any* poem – and he sent them one written 40 years earlier!

He became highly conservative. He celebrated the British Empire devoutly in his verses (and duly despised 'niggers'). Yet he did *not* enjoy secure faith in immortality, which upset him deeply because he really believed that life was meaningless without it. Late in life he dabbled in spiritualism. But he was never a regular churchgoer, despite quiet pressure from his pious wife. It can be argued that the tendency of *In Memoriam* is 'Deistical' rather than strictly Christian; that is, its author believes in God but not in the bases of Christian theology.

He always insisted that *In Memoriam* must not be read as autobiography. It was 'dramatic', he said, and went on, '"I" is not always the author speaking of himself, but the voice of the human race speaking thro' him.' (Quoted in *In Memoriam*, ed. R. H. Ross, p.117.) If *In Memoriam* seems to voice sentiments which are 'typically Victorian', then the 'typically Victorian' speaker was a figure skilfully and painfully constructed amid much doubt and misery by a man almost as eccentric as his delightful friends Edward Lear and Lewis Carroll, and certainly more so than his good-natured, unenvious rival Robert Browning, though the latter wrote rugged, often 'discordant' verse projecting strong sexual passions and obscure ideas.

Browning's fame and success showed that some Victorian readers wanted other things from verse than harmony and reassurance. His verse reminds one that neo-Gothic architecture, the dominant style of the age, often took eclectic and extravagant forms. Even so, the taste of the times was not ready for Gerard Manley Hopkins.

Hopkins, however, born in 1844, was in his private life much more than Tennyson what one thinks of as 'typically Victorian'. He was abstemious and deeply earnest. He had unquestioning Christian faith as well as a deep English patriotism and fervour in respect of the British Empire which was perhaps more extreme even than Tennyson's. Though personally gentle, and often friendly with people who did not share his dogmatic beliefs (which included literal acceptance of miracles), he had the stubborn temperament of a Christian soldier, as hard on sin in himself as in others. Even more than that of the earnest George Eliot, his case supports Gerald Parsons' point that 'Evangelicalism' affected the temperaments of men and women of every religious persuasion.

Hopkins' father, a marine insurer, was a minor poet, and several of Gerard's brothers and sisters were intellectually or artistically very gifted. Gerard, the eldest, wanted to be a painter in early life, and composed music in middle age. In between he proved himself the best student of the classics at Balliol College, Oxford, in his year, 1863. He dismayed his father and tutors by converting to Roman Catholicism, went through arduous training to enter the Jesuit order, and served as parish priest, teacher, and finally as professor of Greek at University College, Dublin, where he died of typhoid in 1889. His intellectual interests were quirky and very diverse, and he would have been only faintly remembered as an inadequate parish priest and unhappy university teacher had he not sent his unpublishable poems to an old Oxford friend, Robert Bridges. Bridges eventually became Poet Laureate, and in 1918 brought out Hopkins' collected verse, which has since been vastly influential wherever poetry has been written in English.

Most of it is marked by technical features which in his lifetime made even Bridges think it 'difficult'. You may yourself have gained this 'difficult' impression when you worked on 'Binsey Poplars' in Units 4–6 *Introduction to Literature*. We are unlikely to be put off now by his use of what he called 'sprung rhythm'. By this, he meant syncopating his verse by juxtaposing stressed syllables – common in ordinary speech, but incompatible with orthodox metres. He was not the first

Figure 12 Gerard Manley Hopkins, aged 30 years. (Source: Photography Collection Harry Ransom Humanities Research Center, University of Texas at Austin, Texas)

English poet to do this, and many writers since 1930 have copied him. But Hopkins also departed frequently from normal word order; he used rare words, and coined new ones; and he felt on occasion compelled to mark stresses where readers might otherwise miss them. So his poems still look and sound unique.

Exercise

Please now turn to Hopkins's sonnet 'Felix Randal', written in 1880, which you will find on page 61 of *Broadcast Notes 2*. Read it through at least once — try reading it aloud.

Discussion

Hopkins's subject-matter here was fresh, yet typical of his own Victorian period. Celebration of the dignity of labour had always been possible within the 'pastoral' tradition. Victorians such as Dickens, Carlyle and the painter Ford Madox Brown had accorded it to the urban workman. Now, thirteen years after the Second Reform Act had given some working men the vote, Hopkins writes elegiacally about an urban blacksmith in the sonnet form formerly used for idealistic love poetry and prophetic comment on high religious and political themes. Randal was an individual parishioner of Hopkins when he worked as a parish priest in Liverpool. But he also serves as a type ('mould') of the 'hardy-handsome' working man — and of mankind in general. Likewise, Hopkins, while expresing personal emotion in a highly individual way, represents, in his relations with Randal the duties of the parish priest. Duty, not accident or attraction, led him to Randal.

    There was nothing archaic in 1880 about the use of 'farrier' for 'blacksmith', which might just have struck you as odd. Denoting 'one who shoes horses', it alliterates usefully with 'Felix'. Alliteration on 'dead . . . duty . . . ended' also features in the first line. As my own *ph*rasing exemplifies, it is actually hard *not* to alliterate *f*requently in written and spoken English. So what is significant, here, in Hopkins's exploitation of this ready-made feature of language?

    It affects the structure of the poem, as we shall see, as well as rhythm and emphasis in individual lines. Compare Hopkins's first line with sentences equivalent in meaning. 'Is Felix Randal the farrier dead? Is my duty towards him completely finished?' Hopkins's choice and ordering of words is much closer to everyday speech, surely — to a spontaneous uttered reaction? We might imagine that someone has just brought the news. '*Felix Randal* (taking it in) *the farrier* (that particular Randal) *O* (exclamation, perhaps grief) *is he dead then?* (still taking it in) *my duty* (I might have paid him a routine visit today) *all* (nothing more can be done now) *ended.*' Alliteration, in this case, slows utterance down, adds emphasis and gravity. (In other cases — be warned! — it serves very different effects. Look at that racing, rushing sonnet, 'Spring'.) What follows is not so much like everyday utterance. But Hopkins is not thinking solely in everyday terms. He is meditating upon the end of a life of craftsmanly labour which has been individual yet archetypal. Our common expression, 'After they made old So-and-So, they threw away the mould', plays on the use of moulds from ancient times in the manufacture of pots, castings, and so on. 'Mould', applied to Randal, suggests 'archetype', 'model'. Yet the word also refers to decay, the process which his body has suffered and which will now continue in the grave. Randal's earthly body and even his reason have been 'broken' by four different diseases 'fleshed' in him. But through 'being anointed', receiving the priest's ministrations, he has 'mended', spiritually. Hopkins, hearing his confession and giving him absolution had 'tendered' — offered — to him the gift of reprieve for sinners from damnation made by Christ through His crucifixion when His blood 'ransomed' humanity. The verb 'tender' suggests the adjective, and thus human fellow-feeling in the priest.

The prayer in line 8 could be rephrased as 'God give him rest despite all the ways in which he sinned'. But 'all road ever' is a much more intimate way of putting it. This is a phrase from Lancashire dialect speech, such as working-man Randal might himself have used. Hopkins goes beyond formal duty into identification with his flock. Line 9 is more than a comfortable truism such as: 'We as priests are drawn into affectionate feeling towards the sick, who in turn feel affection for us.' 'Dear' also refers to cost. The *value* of both parties is enhanced by the emotional transaction. Hence the keen discomfort — like grief — communicated by the unexpected use of 'had' in line 10. We might read a mere statement of fact — '(Before you died) my tongue had . . .' But we sense, I think, uncertainty. So often we say, 'I wish that I had done x, y or z . . .' or 'If only I had . . .' The emotion of the poem is by now very complex (as emotions caused by death usually are). Formally, the priest stands in relation to parishioner as father to child. But the last three lines of the sonnet transform Randal from crying child to hero.

'In your prime, how far you and others were from foreboding that you would die.' Hopkins's inversion of normal word order renders powerful what would otherwise be a trite observation. The Oxford English Dictionary defines 'boisterous' as 'abounding in rough but good natured activity, bordering on excess'. 'Random' is a good example of Hopkins's flair for combining precise denotation with strong connotation. It reinforces the idea that Randal had some wildness in his character, but as a technical term denotes that the forge was constructed of stones of various shapes and sizes. 'Grim' likewise evokes both the forge's rugged and severe aspect, and the hard character of the blacksmith's battering work. 'Peers' literally denotes 'fellow blacksmiths'. But its connotation, 'peers of the realm' is relevant — the farrier in his own sphere is like a lord, 'powerful'. The 'great gray drayhorse' is an awesome client. See how 'sprung rhythm' works here — three consecutive stressed syllables, assonating 'ays' for still greater emphasis. The bright shoe which the smith has battered goes on to batter in its turn paved or cobbled streets, macadamized roads. Why 'sandal', not 'shoe'? The heroes of Homer's *Iliad* wore sandals. So did Christ and His disciples. The word has both epic and sacred connotations. The dead working man is given cosmic status.

'Ah but', I hear you saying, 'surely it's "sandal" merely to rhyme with "Randal"? Hopkins is just picking words which suit the sonnet's rhyme scheme.' To which I'd rejoin, 'That's just what any poet has to do.' Hopkins in fact goes way beyond the necessary minimum in patterning the sounds of words. 'Random' makes an internal half rhyme with both 'Randal' and 'sandal' and echoes back to earlier words — 'handsome', 'ransom'. 'Fore thought', 'fettle' and 'forge' likewise alliterate with 'Fatal four', 'fleshed' — and 'Felix'. Such patterns draw the fourteen lines together as a sustained burst of verbal energy. It's as if Randal's name is a musical motif subjected to aural variations. Since the sharp 'a' of its first syllable is like the 'battering' noise of his trade, the effect is what scholars of medieval verse call 'sound symbolism', otherwise known as 'onomatopoeia'.

The profound and complex human feeling engendered in the poem is activated, not distorted, by Hopkins's highly patterned use of such elements of language as onomatopoeia, alliteration and assonance. All are frequently present in everyday speech, but they are concentrated by him at a more memorable level of utterance. And, as always in his poetry, they are dedicated to the glory of God. Hopkins, after his conversion, wrote almost nothing which did not clearly serve the expression of dogmatic Roman Catholicism.

Exercise

Please now re-read 'Binsey Poplars' and read 'Pied Beauty' and 'Hurrahing in Harvest' (extract II.15 in the Reader). How would you characterize the religious vision which they express? What is striking about it?

Discussion

'Binsey Poplars' might not have struck you as 'religious' at all. It could pass as an unusually intense (even rather hysterical) 'nature' poem. The heavy alliteration and assonance, and the emphatic repetitions help to create a sense of desperation.

Why get so upset about the demise of a few trees? After all, people have used trees for furniture, carts, firewood and so on from time immemorial. It's surely absurd to suggest that any change in 'country' is as drastic as the blinding of an eye. And there's a kind of madness suggested by the first word, 'my', as we re-read the poem. These 'aspens' have special meaning for the speaker of the poem, who reacts like a child dispossessed of a favourite toy.

The poem makes serious sense – of an indirect, 'symbolic' kind – only in relation to ideas displayed in other Hopkins poems. 'Pied Beauty' gets us started on providing the necessary context. This is a poem of praise to God for everything we see in the countryside, both natural and human, praised as 'dappled', then as 'counter, original, spare, strange'. For Hopkins (as for many other poets) what we might dismiss as punning was a marvellous device for enriching a poem's significance. 'Counter' means both 'contrary' (as in 'Mary, Mary...') and, as a noun, 'token' (of God's beauty). 'Spare' means both 'slim, attenuated' (like a poplar) and 'in reserve', like uncultivated ground. Eccentricity and something like wilfulness, *individuality*, and *variety* and *changeability* are praised as the products of a God whose beauty is 'past change'.

So the point of '*Binsey* Poplars' is suggested by the place name. These are *special* poplars, associated with their volatile shadows, their particular relationship (being exactly where they were) to the 'leaping' sun. The world is filled not only with human personalities, like the blacksmith Randal, but with natural individualities. To lose one of these is like bereavement or blinding. To celebrate one of these is to praise God. The 'sweet especial scene' manifests Him.

You may have thought by now of a point of comparison and contrast with Tennyson. Whereas the older poet was deeply dismayed by the idea of an 'individual' human perishing forever, Hopkins reacts as if 'personality' is there in natural growing things. Tennyson's 'individualism' is 'liberal', concerned with the freewill of active people who can change their own destiny, and change nature. (Look again at *In Memoriam*, section 118.) Hopkins's is 'conservative' in so far as it assimilates man with nature – both are as God made them, correctly – and yet it is almost anarchic, 'pantheistic' in its identification of God with every fraction of 'nature'. Paradoxes dissolve if one realizes that for Hopkins, Christ was incarnated in the whole of nature, which is human through His presence. He is not Tennyson's 'Christ-to-be', but Christ *now*.

'Hurrahing in Harvest' depends on this identification. Responding rapturously to natural beauty, 'the beholder' has an experience of Christ, who gives 'replies' which are 'realer' and 'rounder' than any mortal looks and lips. This is a 'feeling' response to nature to which 'science' is utterly irrelevant. (Hopkins, a very precise observer, contributed short accounts of atmospheric phenomena to the scientific weekly, *Nature*. However, his notion of a landscape that testifies to the existence of a heavenly providence is pre-Darwinian.)

Hopkins, theorizing about art and verse, as he often did, coined two new terms, 'inscape' and 'instress'. 'Inscape' was the form or design unique to a given entity – poem, bird, building, man, group of poplars, autumn vista. 'Instress' is the force which preserves inscape, permitting a thing to cohere in its own 'especial' nature, to 'selve' itself – and it is also the force which unites the 'beholder' with what he sees.

Hopkins was not very original in this theorizing. He had wallowed in youth in the works of John Ruskin, whom you have just met in section 6. The fanatical attention to detail in some characteristic Pre-Raphaelite painting anticipates Hopkins. Ruskin had extolled the crucial importance of the 'innocent eye' for the artist, who must make minute observation of the 'infinite variety' of forms in nature. But within the artist, aesthetic and moral energy transform the forms which are seen into art. ALL GREAT ART IS PRAISE, Ruskin insisted. Hopkins was 'Ruskinian' in identifying art with worship and nature with the divine.

But of any vision which sets so much store by 'nature' we must ask the question 'Where does "nature" end?' How can Hopkins logically combine detestation of tree-felling with praise for 'all trades'; carpentry and lumbering are skilled and traditional crafts, after all. The answer is that he can't. He shares with Ruskin and with countless earnest contemporaries an irrational deep suspicion of industrialization, and as a Catholic dogmatist, falls into the dubious habit of equating unpleasant townscapes with sin. 'God made the country but man made the town', another poet once wrote. Yet God made man.

Exercise

Please now read 'God's Grandeur', extract II.15 in the Course Reader.

Discussion

The last four lines of this superbly expressed sonnet recall section 95 of *In Memoriam*, but Hopkins, strict theologian, finds consolation not in the light of the sky as such but in the Holy Ghost informing that light, the 'instress' of its 'inscape'.

Exercise

Now read 'The Starlight Night' (Course Reader, II.15).

Discussion

In this exuberant sonnet, the dogmatism is as obvious as the amazing vigour of the language ('shocks' is a marvellous 'pun', referring both to the gathered bundles of wheat – the souls harvested by Christ – and to the 'shock' which we would receive if we could see Christ, His Mother, and His Saints). The faith of this poem, and its mode of expression seem, in a very positive way, 'childlike'.

Exercise

But now look at 'Duns Scotus's Oxford' (Course Reader, II.15).

Units 18–19 Religion: Conformity and Controversy

Discussion

Hopkins briefly returned to Oxford as a priest twelve years after his days as a student there. He was displeased by the growth of suburbs – 'a base and brickish skirt' on the out 'skirts' of the town where it had once met the 'country'. There is nothing 'childlike' – but nothing 'mature' either – in the petulant expression of crusty conservative feeling in the first eight lines (octet) of the sonnet. As in several sonnets, though, Hopkins turns from observation, 'beholding', to theology in the last six lines, 'sestet'. Here he celebrates Duns Scotus, a fourteenth-century theologian who gave him a more credit-worthy Roman Catholic basis for certain theories than the Protestant Ruskin. Scotus distinguished between general nature and the particular *haeccitas* – 'thisness', 'inscape' – of individual persons and things.

Hopkins was a scrupulously honest and thoughtful man who was nevertheless firm in dogmatic beliefs. Doubt was not his problem. Scotus gave him the authority he wanted so that he could trust his own religious vision. Why was his life so unhappy? Repressed homosexuality is a frequent, but not at all adequate explanation; examples of happy celibates abound. Nor is it enough to argue that there was a conflict between his desire for fame as a poet (and composer? and scholar?) and his priestly commitment to subordination of the self; other gifted Jesuits had, and have since, got round that one. Perhaps the explanation must be found in the effect on his manic-depressive temperament (wild joy swinging to despair) of the situation which he encountered at Oxford as an undergraduate. The fate of England – indeed of the world – seemed to depend on the controversy there.

As a Balliol man he was taught by Jowett, the contributor to *Essays and Reviews*, and Hopkins admired his purity of character. As a confirmed ritualist, he gravitated to Christ Church and Pusey. The epic battle between High and Broad Church was fought to a kind of standstill during Hopkins' years as a student, with the great John Henry Newman sitting, not so much on the sidelines as at a vantage point, in his Oratory in Birmingham. Hopkins never wavered in belief in God. But while Pusey was fighting a rearguard battle (for causes you've learnt about in section 4), dismayed by frequent defections from his camp to his old ally Newman, Jowett, who would emerge with the spoils of war (including the Mastership of Balliol) was nevertheless being maimed by the controversy, so that he avoided disputes thereafter. Young Hopkins had to choose, epically, with an earnestness matching that of his heroes. He wasn't drawn to Roman Catholicism by his aesthetic proclivities – he thought that the Church's trappings were in bad taste. Logic took him there; he accepted Newman's assertion that the real contest was between Roman Catholicism and atheism. Pusey was a 'half-way house' to the first, Jowett to the second. The choice was inevitable, yet agonizing, despite the eventual acceptance of it by his family, and left Hopkins contending with the fearful possibility that he was unworthy of his chosen path. His spirituality, keyed up at Oxford, was too strenuous for his over-sensitive temperament.

However, orthodoxy helped him to produce great poetry about despair, a state familiar to poets and theologians in the Christian tradition. If his despair, in his so-called 'Terrible Sonnets', written in Dublin towards the end of his brief life, is less 'human' than Tennyson's 'honest doubt', it derives tragic grandeur from his complete faith, as a devout Catholic, in God, in tension with his deep conviction, as a 'Victorian', that his own individuality mattered.

Exercise

Please now read 'Carrion Comfort', 'No Worst . . .' and 'Thou Art Indeed Just' (Course Reader, II.15).

Discussion

These are 'orthodox' sonnets of the Petrarchan type in their overall shape. They are 'orthodox' in their religious stance, in so far as it was traditionally permissible to exhaust and correct such feelings by expressing them. The 'anvil' is 'age old'. But it would be indecent to suggest that all that is going on in these poems is just a fresh verbal patterning, an exercise. The 'freshness' is too startling, the voice too 'individual', created through rhythms and diction which may remind us of Shakespeare and Herbert and Milton (three Protestant heretics whose works Hopkins adored) but which tortuously convey to us a sense of intimacy with feelings of torture. These poems demonstrate the old and obvious truth that religious certainty doesn't always make people happy.

REFERENCES

Arnold, M. (1869) *Culture and Anarchy*, London.

Bailey, V. (1977) 'Salvation Army riots: The "Skeleton Army" and legal authority in the provincial town' in A. P. Donajgrodzki, *Social Control in Nineteenth Century Britain*, Croom Helm.

Basalla, G. *et al.* (1970) *Victorian Science*, Doubleday Anchor.

Best, G. (1979) *Mid-Victorian Britain 1851–75*, Fontana.

Boon, B. (1978) *Sing the Happy Song: A History of Salvation Army Vocal Music*, Salvationist Publishing and Supplies.

Darwin, F. (ed.) (1887, 2nd edn.) *The Life and Letters of Charles Darwin*, 3 vols., Murray.

Forrest, D. W. (1974) *Francis Galton*, Elek.

Golby, J. (ed.) (1986) *Culture and Society in Britain 1850–1890: a source book of contemporary writings*, Oxford University Press (referred to in the text as the Course Reader).

Pearson, K. (1937. First published 1892) *The Grammar of Science*, Everyman.

Peel, J. D. Y. (1971) *Herbert Spencer, the Evolution of a Naturalist*, London.

Pointon, M. 'The representation of time in painting: a study of William Dyce's *Pegwell Bay: a recollection of October 5 1858*', *Art History*, 1978, Vol. I, pp.99–103.

Ricks, C. (1972) *Tennyson*, Macmillan.

Ross, R. H. (ed.) (1973) *Alfred, Lord Tennyson, In Memoriam*, Norton (NY).

Ruskin, J. (1856) *Modern Painters*, Vol. III (references in text quoted from the second edition in small form, 1898, George Allen).

Temperley, N. (1979) *The Music of the English Parish Church*, Cambridge University Press.

Tennyson, C. (1949) *Alfred Tennyson*, Macmillan.

Turner, F. M. 'Rainfall, plagues and the Prince of Wales: a chapter in the conflict of religion and science', *Journal of British Studies*, 1973–4, Vol. XII, pp.46–65.

Webb, B. (1926) *My Apprenticeship*, London.

Wilkinson, A. (1978) *The Church of England and the First World War*, SPCK.

Wilson, L. G. (ed.) (1970) *Sir Charles Lyell's Scientific Journals on the Species Question*, Yale University Press.

Units 20–21

MORAL VALUES AND THE SOCIAL ORDER

1 Introduction	73
2 Best on the social order of mid-Victorian Britain	74
2.1 The 'dominant ideology' thesis	75
2.2 Best on 'the social theory of removable inequalities'	76
3 Respectability, independence and the working poor	78
3.1 The working poor in *Hard Times*	79
3.2 Art and work	82
3.3 Evangelicalism, poverty and respectability	89
3.4 The gospel of work	92
4 Roles and representations of women	94
4.1 A conventional view of the role of women	94
4.2 Images of women in Pre-Raphaelite painting	95
4.3 The place of women: representations of the ideal in literature	100
4.4 Religion and attitudes to women	105
5 Critics of the Victorian social order	106
5.1 John Stuart Mill and 'removable inequalities'	107
5.2 Karl Marx	112
5.3 F. D. Maurice and Christian socialism	114
5.4 John Ruskin and William Morris	115
6 Concluding remarks	119
References	120

Contributors

Briony Fer has written Sections 3.2, 4.2 and 5.4; Susan Meikle has written Sections 3.1 and 4.3, and Gerald Parsons has written Sections 3.3 and 4.4 as well as contributing to Section 5.3. Stuart Brown has co-ordinated the material and written the remaining sections. He was particularly helped by discussions with Gordon Clark, a postgraduate student of the Open University, on whose research material Section 5.2 is based.

Units 20–21 Moral Values and the Social Order

SET READING

As you work through these units you will need to refer to
Geoffrey Best (1979) *Mid-Victorian Britain 1851–75* (Set Book)
John Golby (ed.) (1986) *Culture and Society in Britain 1850–1890* (Course Reader)
Charles Dickens (1989 edition) *Hard Times* (Set Book)
Supplementary Material booklet
Illustration booklet
Cassette Notes
Broadcast Notes

BROADCASTING

Television programme 20 *Religion and Society in Victorian Bristol*
Television programme 21 *Victorian Views of the Art of the Past*
Radio programme 10 *George Eliot: A Search for Secular Answers*

CASSETTE

Cassette 4, side 1, band 2 *Women Artists and Writers*

1 INTRODUCTION

The moral and social values of a society are usually expressed directly or indirectly in various kinds of writing, including sermons, novels, philosophical essays and social commentaries. They are also embodied – sometimes more powerfully – in its painting, architecture and music. By looking at these and other products of a particular age we can find out something about its moral and social values. More broadly, we often have access to other kinds of information about past societies, for instance about how property was distributed, what rights and privileges were granted to what classes of people, and so on. Various kinds of changes – in where people lived, how they made their livings, what rights the law of the land conferred on them – are all changes in what we call the 'social order'.

The moral and social values of a society tend to be enshrined in its social order in various ways. One obvious way is in that part of the social order which is controlled by legislation. To take a simple example, the law may say that wives are the 'dependents' of their husbands. This may mean different things but in Britain during some part of the nineteenth century it meant that, while men were required to provide for their wives, married women were debarred from holding property in their own right. Although the subordinate place of women was being challenged in Victorian Britain, to the extent that legislation is unopposed in a society, it may correspond with widely held moral and social values, at least amongst those with political power. The social inequalities between men and women as confirmed by law may be expected to correspond with different ideals of behaviour. Gentlemen may be expected, amongst other things, to protect members of the 'weaker' sex. Ladies, on the other hand, may be expected to be demure and submissive, allowing men to make the decisions.

So far, I hope, it will seem obvious to you that there will be some connection between the moral values of a society and its social order. But how is that connection established? It might seem that people first 'decide on' their moral and social values and then shape society accordingly. But major social changes are often not intended by anybody. No individual decided and no group of individuals got together to decide that there should be the massive shift in population from the country to the town that occurred in nineteenth-century Britain. Even in the case of the emancipation of women, it might be argued that the position of women was changed more as an unintended consequence of the First World War, when women were recruited in large numbers to do work previously reserved for men, than by the efforts of right-thinking people.

In these units we shall be looking at moral and social values as they are expressed in the works of various writers and artists of our period. We shall try to see how these values related to the prevailing social order. I say 'various writers and artists' but obviously our time is too limited to engage in any kind of comprehensive study. What we are going to do is to look at a particular thesis which has commended itself to a number of historians, including Professor Geoffrey Best, author of one of our set books, *Mid-Victorian Britain 1851–75*. Best concurs with the view of those historians who see the mid-Victorian period as a period of relative calm between times of social unrest. If he is right then the earlier part of our period is one of comparative social stability. What makes Best's thesis of particular interest is that he also claims that there was (in the period 1851–70) a high degree of consensus about fundamental moral and social values which helped to make it 'an age of equipoise'. That consensus was beginning to break down in the 1870s, according to Best, and late Victorian society became much more fragmented.

Best's picture of the relations between the moral values of the mid-Victorians and the social order of their time invites three groups of questions, which we shall be addressing in these units:

1   How far was there a consensus about moral and social values during our period and to what extent did it begin to disintegrate towards the end?

2   How were subordinate groups like women and poor working people regarded? To what extent were they invited to think of themselves in terms of the same values as others?

3   How far were there alternative sets of values being advocated during our period? How radically different were they? How influential were they?

We shall be concerned throughout these units with how far Best's claims are borne out by a study of paintings as well as literary, philosophical and religious writings. But first of all let us consider Best's claims in greater detail.

2 BEST ON 'THE SOCIAL ORDER OF MID-VICTORIAN BRITAIN'

Before we proceed further I suggest you re-read Chapter 4 of Professor Best's book. It is entitled 'The Social Order of Mid-Victorian Britain'.

Exercise

Read all of the chapter, if you have time, but please pay particular attention to pp. 250–9 and the sections entitled 'Respectability and Independence' (pp. 279–86) and 'Social Dissidence' (pp. 286–92). As you work through the chapter, make notes towards an answer to the following questions:

1   What ideas, according to Best, were of particular importance in maintaining a sense of social harmony between different classes in mid-Victorian Britain?

2   How do you see these ideas as related to one another?

3   To what extent, according to Best, did social critics ('dissidents') of the day challenge these ideas?

Discussion

1   At one point Best says that social harmony in mid-Victorian Britain 'rested on a common acceptance by (as it seemed) the greater part of every articulate social group, of a hierarchical social order, and on the wide diffusion of a common cult of personal qualities known as "respectability" and "independence"' (p. 254). Later he introduces the 'removable inequalities' theory and suggests that it, together with the practice of deference and the concept of a gentleman, served to make an unequal society acceptable and thus to reduce social tension (p. 279).

2   These ideas are linked together in an uneasy way to give the appearance of reconciling *élitist* qualities (ones only attainable by a few) with more *universal* qualities. The possession of social rank and the deference which goes with it was the property of an élite. The qualities of independence and respectability, however, could be cultivated even by the poor and were therefore more universal. The 'removable inequalities' theory implies that the cultivation of certain

virtues (respectability, independence, etc.) could lead, at least in exceptional cases, to ordinary people being elevated in rank. (See especially the report of a Palmerston speech quoted by Best on pp. 256–8.) The privileges of rank are thus, in principle, to be thought of as universally accessible. In a rather different way the idea of a gentleman was invoked to bridge the divisions between classes. For while, in reality, a gentleman was someone enjoying a more than middling position in the social hierarchy, the qualities of gentlemanly conduct were universal so that, in a certain sense, it could be claimed that anyone – or at least any man – could be a gentleman.

3 Best does not deny that there were social critics who challenged these values. He says that Ruskin, for example, was 'applauded and ignored' (p. 289). Those who could not be ignored, like the middle and upper-class Liberal politicians who helped to lead popular radicalism, 'had one and all done so on the understanding that their working-class radical friends and supporters cared as much for independence and respectability and removable inequalities as they did...' (p. 289). Socialist values of comradeship made little impact, according to Best, until the 1880s (p. 250).

2.1 THE 'DOMINANT IDEOLOGY' THESIS

A set of ideas which serves to foster social cohesion is commonly called an 'ideology'. The word 'ideology' is used in a number of ways, some of them very loose. A precise use would need to be linked to a precise theory about how moral and social values are linked to the social order. According to one theory, for example, the groups which dominate in society try to maintain their dominance by making *their* values acceptable to subordinate groups, by a systematic (conscious or unconscious) misrepresentation of social relationships. In this way it is possible to maintain an unequal society in which those who are subordinate comply without needing to be threatened or coerced. The ideology by which their compliance is thus secured would be what is called a 'dominant ideology'.

Professor Best does not make any use of the word 'ideology' and the fact that he prefers not to use it indicates some underlying disagreements between him and those who do. (See *Introduction to History*, Unit 1, Section 7.) But those who have put forward what is called the 'dominant ideology thesis' about mid-Victorian Britain put forward a quite similar thesis to his. Like Best they have been concerned to explain why the 1850s and 1860s were relatively stable years for British society in spite of the fact that conditions for the majority of people were hard if not harsh (see Best, p. 279). Their accounts, like Best's, invoke a set of ideas that helped to preserve social harmony by making the existence of privilege and wealth more acceptable to those who had neither.

There are none the less important differences of detail on which it is good for us to keep an open mind. It is not entirely clear how widely such an ideology was shared, and it has been maintained by some that the really down-trodden and needy were quite uninfluenced by it. Best himself only claims that there was 'a common acceptance by (as it seemed) the greater part of every articulate social group of a hierarchical social order' (p. 254) and this is consistent with there being a (so to speak) passively resisting class who had quite different values. Indeed, Best's reference to 'a proletarian culture of comradeship, improvidence and good cheer' (p. 291) shows his willingness to admit this may be so.

There is also some controversy as to the explanation for the consensus about moral and social values which is commonly supposed to have existed at this time. For a consensus may be achieved without its being a matter of one group succeeding in imposing its way of thinking on others. The dominant ideology thesis will commend itself to those who are inclined to believe that the interests of the middle and working classes were essentially antagonistic. But it could be that some working-class men were entirely reasonable in believing that they were likely to be better off in the hierarchical society they knew than they would be in any practicable alternative. Like the rising middle classes, the rising working classes could be optimistic about their future and at all events had too much to lose by throwing in their lot with those who worked for revolution. Their shared ideology might reflect a shared interest in supporting the existing social order with all its inequalities and injustices rather than seeking to undermine it.

For this reason the word 'ideology' does not always carry with it the implication that certain ideas are spread in the interests of a powerful minority. Indeed, it is sometimes used of sets of values that unite sub-groups within a society. A society might be divided into classes with competing interests and therefore with competing ideologies. In such a society there might be little or no consensus about values. But historians who have written about British society in the mid-Victorian period have been struck by the absence of class conflict at that time. What is remarkable about this apparent harmony between social classes is that it existed at a time when exploitation and discrimination were rife. The dominant ideology thesis is an explanation of how this could have been so.

2.2 BEST ON 'THE SOCIAL THEORY OF REMOVABLE INEQUALITIES'

As we have seen, Best does not use the word 'ideology'. He writes instead, for instance, of 'the social theory of removable inequalities' (p. 258). But this is no ordinary theory. A social theory is usually successful only to the extent that its explanations are *true*. But the success of the theory of 'removable inequalities' was secured merely by its being *believed*. Lord Palmerston (whom Best refers to as 'the dominant politician of the period') is credited with being its 'foremost populariser', of being one of the first to put forward what by 1855 had become 'the standard claptrap of patriotic boosters'. Palmerston, for his part, was a 'master' at putting forward the 'theory' and, for their part, it was 'exactly what Britons wanted to hear' (p. 255). Men were rising, so Palmerston claimed in what Best refers to as a 'rhapsody', from the lowest to the highest points of the social ladder. The implication of Palmerston's speech (quoted in Best, pp. 255–8) is that he believed this was a new and peculiarly British trend and, indeed, that it was one he welcomed. But Best hints that we should not take what Palmerston said at its face value. It is, on the contrary, a masterly piece of rhetoric whose achievement consists in putting across an untruth in such a way as to make it seem plausible. Palmerston, in short, was engaged in manipulating the working men who were presented at the prize-giving of the South London Industrial Exhibition.

You might think this is a rather cynical portrayal of Palmerston. But let us look at the promise he made at the climax of his speech:

> You may not all become Generals or Admirals; you may not all become Lord Chancellors or Archbishops; you may not become members of the Cabinet; but depend upon it, you will, by systematic industry, raise yourselves in the social system of your country . . .' (Best, p. 258)

Exercise

What sort of reason do you think we might have for doubting whether Palmerston actually believed that mid-Victorian society was one in which people would, and should, advance on merit, in virtue of 'systematic industry'?

Discussion

One reason might be that it was so obviously false that Palmerston could not really have believed it. Best presents us with a picture of a hierarchical society in which advancement on merit was a rarity. He cites the Bank official who could declare with pride that the London and Westminster could staff itself with clerks without stooping to include the sons of shopkeepers (p. 273). His point is that obstacles to the advance on merit of people from the lower classes were pervasive in mid-Victorian society. Palmerston invited his audience to believe that these obstacles could sometimes be overcome:

> Look at your Army, your Navy, your Law, your Church, your statesmen. You will find in every one of those careers men who have risen to the highest points, who have either themselves started from the smallest beginnings, or whose fathers began with nothing but their talents, their industry, and their energy to aid them. (Quoted in Best, p. 257)

This is given as evidence for thinking that in Britain working-class men could hope to advance on merit. In other countries, where there are 'aristocracies of wealth and rank', 'there are almost impossible barriers separating them from the rest of the nation'. But, Palmerston roundly declared, 'no such barriers exist in this country' (Best, p. 256). Best implies that this was so obviously false (or at any rate exaggerated to the point of falsehood) that Palmerston could not have believed it. And certainly there is a huge gap between what is supported by the evidence (that the barriers were not absolutely impossible) and the conclusion that Britain was a place where people would advance on merit.

The fact that a conclusion is false (even obviously false) and is by no means supported by the argument in its favour is not by itself a reason to challenge the sincerity of the person who advances it. But it may have occurred to you that politicians are often more frank in their remarks to close associates than they are when making public speeches. If, then, Palmerston was inclined to say exactly the same thing in private we could conclude that he was sincere in his belief that Britain had become a society in which people could advance on merit. If, on the other hand, he said quite contrary things, we should have good reason to doubt his sincerity.

There is, as it happens, evidence of a direct kind to suggest that Palmerston neither believed that in mid-Victorian society the higher ranks were open to all nor that he would have particularly welcomed it. Elsewhere he expresses a commitment to a closed aristocracy, to the idea that some are born into it and are the natural and proper inheritors of wealth and rank. This is implicit in a comment he made in 1865 on the problems of men from the lower classes becoming officers in the Army:

> I think it extremely desirable that the British Army should be officered by gentlemen as a rule... I think, speaking plainly, that in all armies, it is the higher classes that lead the lower classes, and it seldom happens that persons belonging to the lower classes can rise, with comfort to themselves, to a position for which they were not originally destined. (Quoted by Alan Ereira in *The People's England*, p. 80)

Notice that in this remark Palmerston makes no pretence that Britain was any different from other aristocracies except that it sometimes happened that men from the lower classes rose to higher positions. In a way this is not strictly inconsistent with what he said in his 1855 speech, except for the emphasis. In the 1855 speech the possibility of rising in society is offered as an incentive to work and as something to hope for. In these (1865) remarks this possibility is seen as a disruption of the proper order of things and therefore as acceptable only as an occasional exception to the rule that people should stick to the position for which they were 'originally destined'. There is little doubt that in 1865 he was indeed 'speaking plainly' where in 1855 he had been careful to disguise his true feelings.

I have dwelt on the Palmerston speech partly because of the importance Best attaches to it and partly to give you some sense of what a 'dominant ideology' is. It is a form of deception which is spread amongst people by or on behalf of those in power in order to preserve their position. But it has to be something that *can* be believed and which, for some reason, people *want* to believe. If Palmerston had said that Britain was no longer an 'aristocracy of wealth and rank' but now a land of opportunity, he could hardly have hoped to be believed. His artistry lay in conceding the obvious fact but in stressing the difference between Britain and the aristocracies of Europe against whom there had been a series of revolutions in 1848. There were not, in Britain, the 'almost impassible barriers' between the aristocracy and the common people that there were in 'other countries'. Working men in Britain could look to the future with hope and had no need to resort to reckless attempts at overthrowing the established order.

As Best suggests, Palmerston's audience of prize-contending artisans wanted to believe this. Doubtless they hoped that there really was a trend in Britain that would give opportunities for their children of which Palmerston would have privately disapproved. But in the meantime here was a way of thinking that appeared to reconcile their aspirations with the acceptance of the established social order. It is the prevalence of this way of thinking that, according to Best, explains the fact that mid-Victorian Britain was, at least on the surface, a period of calm and relative social harmony.

In order to see how far Best's account is borne out, we shall begin by looking at the way in which working men were represented in the art and in various writings of the period.

3 RESPECTABILITY, INDEPENDENCE AND THE WORKING POOR

You may recall, from Unit 16, that the Great Exhibition was seen as reflecting credit on the British working classes. It was a tribute to the skill of the many workmen who contributed to the exhibits. And the orderly behaviour of the huge crowds who travelled to see the exhibition was a symptom of a new-found 'respectability'. The common man, it seemed, could quietly improve his lot by dint of hard work. And this idea was preached at the working classes in the '50s and '60s. It was a central part of the message of a best-selling book appropriately called *Self-Help* (1859, many later editions).

The author of this book, Samuel Smiles, was one of many middle-class Victorians with a strong commitment to the education and improvement of working-class men. Smiles had given some talks to young working men in the north of England which were so successful that he was persuaded to write them up in book form. He himself says that he addressed these young men on more than one occasion,

> citing examples of what other men had done, as illustrations of what each might, in a greater or lesser degree, do for himself; and pointing out that their happiness and well-being as individuals in afterlife, must necessarily depend mainly on themselves – upon their own diligent self-culture, self-discipline, and self-control – and, above all, on that honest and upright performance of individual duty, which is the glory of manly character. (Smiles, *Self-Help*, 1860 edition, p.v)

Smiles took care to include nothing original or controversial in his advice, which he claimed was 'as old as the Proverbs of Solomon'. There is no hint that the lot of working people might be improved by political action and indeed, as we shall see in Unit 27, Smiles was, in his way, popularizing the same ideas as Palmerston: of acquiescence in the (hierarchical) social order and a cult of 'independence', 'systematic industry' and 'self-help'.

3 Respectability, Independence and the Working Poor

But not all the Victorians were content to be as uncritical or as unoriginal as Smiles. And, while Smiles's *Self-Help* is a good source book for anyone interested in conventional Victorian values, there were also creative minds at work whose attitude to the Victorian social order was rather different. Amongst these, as you will already know from your reading of *Hard Times*, was Charles Dickens.

3.1 THE WORKING POOR IN 'HARD TIMES'

In this section we shall look at how the moral values represented in *Hard Times* relate to the Victorian social values discussed in Section 2 and how far the novel can be said to support dominant beliefs in, for example, 'deference' and 'removable inequalities' which Geoffrey Best suggests characterized mid-Victorian social attitudes (see Best, Chapter 4, pp. 254–5). But first we need to ask if there are particular moral values advocated or criticized by the novel.

Exercise

Write provisional answers to the following questions:

1 Are there attitudes and practices criticized by *Hard Times* and, if so, who represents them?

2 Are there basic moral values we are asked to assent to in the novel and, if so, which characters represent them?

Discussion

It seems to me that there are attitudes attacked in the novel, most especially those embodied in Mr Bounderby, Mr Harthouse and Mrs Sparsit (Bitzer and Young Tom could perhaps qualify more as victims of these attitudes than embodiments of them). The impulse motivating characters like Bounderby and Harthouse could be labelled 'calculated self-interest', but in the guise of rationality or adherence to 'facts'.

In answer to the second question, we could name those characters who are *not* motivated by such self-interest (like Rachael, Stephen Blackpool, Mrs Pegler and Sissy Jupe) as those who embody the positive values of affection and disinterested love. Moreover, these characters are shown to be capable of such affection because they can exercise a sympathetic imagination for the feelings of others. Notice, however, that there is a social division which parallels the moral one: those who most thoroughly reflect these positive moral values are the poor and disenfranchised.

The first character to express these values is Sissy Jupe, who is remarkable for being singularly immune to any influence by the Gradgrind philosophy. Her virtue is succinctly summarized and contrasted with its opposite in the remark that

> after eight weeks of induction into the elements of Political economy, she had . . . been set right by a prattler three feet high, for returning to the question, 'What is the first principle of this science?' the absurd answer, 'To do unto others as I would that they should do unto me.' (p. 73)

Sissy Jupe proves totally uneducable in the 'facts' of Mr Gradgrind's school, but she is seen nevertheless to be a constant nurturing influence in his home and the saviour of his son and daughter. Sissy and her fellow circus performers, as well as the working poor of Coketown, like Stephen Blackpool and Rachael, express qualities such as mercy, goodness and forbearance, which lie at the heart of Christian moral teaching as it is represented, for example, in the Sermon on the Mount. The source of Stephen's virtue and its promise for his fellows are explicitly connected to the Christian message when Stephen gazes at the star from the bottom of the mineshaft and prays that 'aw th' world may o'ny coom together more' (p. 363). The narrator then gives full assent to this hope by associating Stephen's star with the Star of Bethlehem: 'The star had shown him where to find the God of the poor; and through humility, and sorrow, and forgiveness, he had gone to his Redeemer's rest' (p. 365).

Exercise

Between the two moral extremes of Mr Bounderby and Stephen Blackpool stand Mr Gradgrind and Louisa. How do they fit into the moral scheme of the novel? How do they differ in treatment from the other characters we have mentioned?

Discussion

They are the two characters whose progress from one moral position to the other provides the actual drama of the novel, the victory of affection and disinterested love over self-interest. Both Gradgrind and Louisa learn the virtue of sympathetic fellow-feeling, the moral capacity which Dickens links directly with the power of the imagination.

Throughout the novel we are asked to see how allowing the growth of the imagination through art and pleasure is necessary for the development of true fellow-feeling. What is more, Dickens asks us to experience this process working in our own reading of the novel. He engages our own imaginative capacity rather than making the novel's impact felt through rational argument. The simple ways characters look at or stand near fire, for example, become symbolic gestures for their own imaginative potential, and it is our imaginations which register these meanings. We are not *told* what that potential is, but gradually build up an awareness of it through our registering of the actions and imaginatively comparing them as we read the novel. Louisa's constant gazing into the fire, for instance, provides a first clue to her irrepressible urge to 'wonder', to use her imagination, despite outward appearances and her father's attempts to suppress all such irrational urges. When we find Bounderby always standing with his back to the fire, in order to assume a 'commanding position' (p. 19), we can see his action figuratively as the opposite to Louisa, a blunt refusal to wonder at anything. In such a context of symbolic associations, it is then possible to see a significance, which we can perhaps only fully recognize with retrospect, in Mr Gradgrind's staring into the fire on pp. 24ff and asking where Louisa's 'vulgar curiosity' for the circus could have come from. In his stance and question we begin to register how Mr Gradgrind's definition of wonder is wrong and how his own inclination to ask the question while staring into the fire becomes a subtle clue as to his own potential for wonder, and, therefore, for a redemption which will remain lost to the likes of Bounderby.

Having established broadly how the novel criticizes or advocates specific moral values through individual characters, we can now turn to explore how it may be possible to say whether *Hard Times* adheres to those other social values Geoffrey Best says characterized mid-Victorian society, that is, belief in 'removable inequalities' and 'deference'. To review the steps we have taken so far: take the example of Stephen Blackpool, whose actions reveal qualities of both respectability and independence, in accordance with much mid-Victorian thinking (see Best, p. 254).

Exercise

Is there any way the novel suggests that he or his fellow workers can use these qualities to remove the inequalities which separate them from their employers?

Discussion

The novel appears to me neither to prophesy nor to recommend that the inequalities which shape the workers' lives could or should be removed. When we laugh at the absurdity of Bounderby's accusation that workers' protests are merely a disguise for wanting to eat off gold spoons, we are laughing at his outrageous refusal to see the real conditions suffered by his workers. But at the same time, by using this kind of irony against Bounderby, Dickens could also be said to avoid asking questions which probe exactly what conditions do demand remedy.

When it comes to the question whether single individuals should be able to overcome inequalities of birth or social status, the novel does seem to challenge the notion of 'removable inequalities' in its outright condemnation of Bounderby, the thoroughly 'self-made man' (p. 18). Both he and Bitzer, the only two individuals who exemplify the notion of 'removable inequalities', are shown to deny the ties of human affection and to be motivated solely by their own calculated self-interest. Not only does the moral design of the novel condemn the two characters who represent 'the self-made man', but it also invests the greatest virtues in those who *least* desire to improve themselves socially – those who suffer the greatest inequalities. They are not only virtuous and poor, but accepting of their lot.

Exercise

Yet throughout *Hard Times* there remains an implicit recognition that the lives of the working poor are filled with undeserved suffering. Does the novel suggest that the obvious inequalities between rich and poor can be remedied? Does it propose basic changes in the actual economic structures of Coketown or in the social and economic relations of its inhabitants?

Discussion

It seems to me that from the evidence of the novel the answer to the last question is 'No', and that the overriding conviction is that change can only rightly be effected through waking the moral sensibilities of individual human beings, by encouraging the exercise of their sympathy and imagination. The novel supports neither shifts of power by means of organized union 'combination' on the part of the workers, nor ruthless consolidation of power by the wealthy who treat their workers as so much factory fodder for profit. We are offered instead images of alternative modes of co-operation and a different kind of combination: the world of the circus people, for example, shows how the very lives and well-being of its people depend upon mutual co-operation, and in the rescue scene we are shown how men and women can co-operate and sympathetic impulses bind them into an efficient working force to save human life.

One can argue that because *Hard Times* finally seeks solutions by changes in individual human hearts rather than changes in social structures, it inevitably defers to the political and economic *status quo*, and that it thus conforms to the tendency towards stability cited by Geoffrey Best in Chapter 4 of his book. But to say simply that *Hard Times* fails in the end sufficiently to challenge the *status quo* would be to ignore the persuasiveness of its recognition that human relations do matter and do lie at the heart of what may appear merely to be questions of political power, economic calculation or mechanical efficiency. This emphasis on the quality of individual human experience gives the clue to Dickens's reason for dedicating the novel to Thomas Carlyle. *Hard Times* is itself an echo of Carlyle's accusation in his 'Signs of the Times' (1829) that his world was growing 'mechanical in head and heart, as well as in hand'. But beneath Dickens's desire for peaceful, humane relations between the working poor and their employers there is also a recognizable unease which motivates that wish for peace. We can see, for example, how the tone and language of the narrator's voice urgently express to 'good people of an anxious turn of mind' (p. 91) – who, we assume, are his very readers – that calculation and control are inappropriate when transferred from machines to men. Men, says the narrator, cannot be reduced to 'so many hundred horse Steam Power', but are an 'unfathomable mystery' (p. 92). And underlying this plea, there is also a sense of danger expressed which adds to the urgency in the narrator's voice.

Units 20–21 Moral Values and the Social Order

Exercise

Look, for example, at his address on p. 216 to 'Utilitarian economists, skeletons of schoolmasters, Commissioners of Facts' (the Gradgrinds of mid-Victorian Britain) and note down the argument put forward; what are its premises and its conclusion?

Discussion

There seem to me to be both explicit and implicit premises which could be shown as follows:

Explicit premises

The poor you always have with you.

Their lives are in need of ornament.

Without ornament all romance is driven out of their souls, and they have nothing but a bare existence.

Implicit premises

Those who have power are in a position to triumph over the poor. They also have power to cultivate in them imagination and affection which must be cultivated or...

Conclusion

The bare existence of the poor will be their only 'Reality', and this reality will destroy the powerful.

By putting the argument this way, we have stuck to the 'facts' of the passage, that which can be set down as a rational argument. And this alone expresses grounds for setting right the relations among the classes.

Exercise

But a merely rational analysis of the argument does not register the one striking, emotionally persuasive metaphor at the heart of the passage. What is it? And what is its effect?

Discussion

That 'Reality will take a *wolfish turn* and make an end of you'. The phrase 'wolfish turn' makes its impact not factually, as it were, not literally, but as an image expressing an urgency born of fear that a wild, predatory collective destruction, as of wolves hunting in packs, awaits those who do not attend to the pressing needs of the poor. This single metaphor expresses the danger of powerful 'combination' by the lower classes which Dickens in *Hard Times* and the middle classes of Britain both feared and resisted.

In an article written at the same time as *Hard Times*, called 'On Strike', Dickens refers to the 'mistake' of the strikers and asks if there is not 'some little thing wanting in the relations between them and their employers, which neither political economy nor drum-head proclamation writing will altogether supply, and which we cannot too soon or too temperately unite in trying to find out' (Course Reader, extract IV. 6). As you study *Hard Times* further and relate it to other aspects of these units, consider how far the novel offers the 'missing something' Dickens felt was needed to bring better social relations in nineteenth-century industrial society, and how far his views accord with those of other artists and social critics of the time.

3.2 ART AND WORK

First of all, please turn back to p. 74 and the three questions raised at the beginning of these units. It is question (2) that concerns me here — as I shall be

3 Respectability, Independence and the Working Poor

considering how the working poor could be represented in art. Rather than cover a wide range of paintings, I shall concentrate on Ford Madox Brown's *Work*. This will enable us to look in some depth at the complex relationship between a work of art and the values, attitudes and beliefs that work may express.

But before going any further, I want to make a general point about the way we might approach the representation of the working poor in art. So now look at the reproductions of these works:

1   Ford Madox Brown, *Work* (Colour Plate 29), oil on canvas, 1852–63.

2   Gustave Doré, *Mixing the Malt* (Plate 49); *Lambeth Gasworks* (Plate 47); engravings for *London: A Pilgrimage* published in 1872, with a text by Blanchard Jerrold.

3   Hubert Von Herkomer, *On Strike* (Plate 48), oil on canvas, 1891.

Ford Madox Brown was a close associate of the Pre-Raphaelites, though never one of their number. Doré was a French artist working in London and his engravings for *London: A Pilgrimage* explored the city in many different aspects, with a particular emphasis on the conditions of the urban poor. And from the 1870s, Herkomer worked as an illustrator and painter, particularly concerned with themes of social distress. Many strikes took place during the 1880s and '90s and this work may refer to the Dockers' Strike of 1889. Unlike Herkomer's painting of a striking worker and his family, Brown dealt with a whole range of social types and classes in *Work*. So, in the context of the whole series of *London* engravings, did Doré. Common to all these works was the belief that the lower social ranks were appropriate subjects to be represented.

Exercise

Briefly jot down what strikes you as different, or even odd, in the depiction of figures and setting in Ford Madox Brown's *Work*, in comparison with the other images.

Discussion

What I think is immediately striking in Brown's picture is that the figures in their setting seem deliberately compressed. Yet Brown's means of depiction – with its scrupulous attention to detail – would seem to suggest his aim was to construct a realistic image of contemporary life. He has depicted a range of social types and classes in a particular place, stressing the specific details of dress and location, in 'heightened focus', as it were. And the crampedness of the spatial distribution of the figures draws attention and alerts us to the fact that this is no straightforward reflection of a real scene. It is in fact an allegory of work, but more of that later.

However, as you will know from your study of the *Introduction to Art History*, Units 10–12, no representation is the straightforward reflection of reality. Doré, for instance, has used the device of distortion, the contrast of light and shade and other artistic conventions to construct his graphic image. Herkomer is often seen as a social realist whose art objectively recorded and documented poverty. It is easy to see why – there are no obvious artistic flourishes in his picture: it is dour and austere. We shall return to the work of Herkomer and Doré in Units 29–30. The point I want to stress here is that the Herkomer is no more a 'mirror image' of the world than the other images we are looking at, or somehow 'truer'; rather, Herkomer contrived that effect through his use of the artistic medium. Images, then, are not transparent, impartially reflecting the world or its values: they are constructed accorded to certain skills and conventions. The question of 'true' or 'false' pictures is not applicable.

With these points in mind, let us now consider Ford Madox Brown's *Work* in terms of contemporary ideas about labour and how labour could be represented in art during the 1850s and '60s. Although *Work* was begun in 1852, it was not completed until 1863. The artist saw the painting as his 'magnum opus' and exhibited it as the centrepiece of a retrospective show at a gallery in Piccadilly in

1865. He had taken a great deal of time over the picture and held great store by it. He also wrote a lengthy account of *Work* to accompany its exhibition.

Exercise

Now read Brown's account (extract III. 6 in the Course Reader). As you do so, refer back to Colour Plate 29 and identify the figures Brown describes.

1 Who are the central figures depicted in *Work*?
2 What kind of work does Brown claim they represent?
3 What other kinds of work are compared?

Discussion

1 The central figures in *Work* are the five navvies. The *hero* of the piece is the British navvy or excavator, represented in terms of various types: the old, the young and so forth.

2 They represent manual and physical labour. Brown saw the navvy as 'the outward and visible type of *Work*'.

3 The major comparison is drawn between physical labour and 'brainwork' represented by the two male figures standing on the right: these, 'seeming to be idle, work, and are the cause of well-ordained work and happiness in others'. The 'idle rich' or those who need not work are set against the manual and intellectual workers.

Ford Madox Brown had derived these ideas from Thomas Carlyle, to whom Dickens had dedicated, as you may remember, *Hard Times*. Carlyle had not envisaged the need for a new structure to society, but he had fiercely criticized its social relationships 'with cash payment as the sole nexus'. In *Past and Present* Carlyle had attacked the *laissez-faire* system (discussed further on page 111 below). He saw work as sacred, elevated to a heroic and dignified status. Each kind of work was believed to be worthy of a respected place in the social fabric (see below, Section 3.4). The interesting point here is that Carlyle's ideas of the 1840s were clearly seen by Ford Madox Brown as still appropriate to his contemporary society – which casts some doubt on Best's insistence on social consensus. Rather than a regressive feature, aspects of Carlyle's critique continued to be seen as relevant by many.

Ford Madox Brown includes a portrait of Carlyle (*cf.* Fig. 1) as one of his 'brainworkers' on the right of the picture, but does not mention him by name in the text. Indeed, we need to locate that commentary historically, just as we do the work itself. It was written after the painting was completed so we should not imagine that the artist had these ideas in this order, which he then went about translating into visual form. And as a piece of art, *Work* is not merely an illustration of ideas that exist external to it: ideas are expressed, rather than reflected, in the painting.

The way meanings are produced in the painting depends on the artist's use of the material, both technical and ideological, at his disposal. Here Brown has used the traditional tool of *allegory*. In the allegory of *Work* the seemingly natural elements of the scene serve as emblems for the abstract idea of work. This is signalled by the nature of the composition we looked at earlier. Allegorical personifications were common currency during this period. Look, for instance, at two examples from the 1851 Great Exhibition catalogue – the title page and a design for a pediment illustrated in Figures 2 and 3; or at the way 'science' and 'art' appear as idealized, classically draped figures in the trade-union banner of The Operative Society of Bricklayers (Colour Plate 28, originally designed in c. 1865 and discussed in television programme 23). Ford Madox Brown's use of this device is very different: there are no 'timeless' classical robes present in *Work*. He has clothed the idea of work in the carefully observed contemporary figure of the navvy.

3 Respectability, Independence and the Working Poor

Figure 1   Photograph of Carlyle by unidentified photographer. Ford Madox Brown could not get Carlyle to sit for his portrait in Work *so had this photograph taken of him, probably in 1858. (Photo: Birmingham City Art Gallery)*

Units 20–21 Moral Values and the Social Order

Figure 2 Title-page edition of the Art Journal Illustrated Catalogue to the Great Exhibition, 1851. *Art and industry are personified in the two kneeling male figures, surrounded by their attributes, and united by the central female figure who holds the attributes of peace, victory and purity. Note that none of the figures is depicted in contemporary dress.*

Figure 3 Pediment designed by C. Fox. *'The subject is intended to represent the "Arts, Commerce and Manufactures, promoted by the Great Exhibition". The first group to the left represents Navigation, the next industry bringing her offerings to Peace. In the centre is the Queen, holding out wreaths of laurel to the various contributors, and to the right the Fine Arts and Science are symbolised in respective groups.' (Photo and description from the* Art Journal Illustrated Catalogue to the Great Exhibition, 1851*)*

3 Respectability, Independence and the Working Poor

Exercise

Briefly, how would you characterize the different depictions of manual labour in *Work* and Millais's *Christ in the Carpenter's Shop* (Colour Plate 21)?

Discussion

First and foremost, the contemporary, secular setting for manual labour in *Work* contrasts with the biblical context of Joseph's workshop. Though in Millais's painting the humble work of the carpenter is depicted as sacred, it is not the main subject of the painting (remember we discussed how the picture related to contemporary religious controversy in Units 18–19). For Brown, the idea of the sacredness of work could equally be represented in the context of modern life.

The navvies occupy the central and conventionally the most important part of the composition, representing the heroic nature of manual labour in the foreground. This treatment of the lower social ranks is monumental when compared with the way the poor had traditionally been represented in the painting of *genre* or everyday life (see Plate 23 and compare scale and intention). In *Introduction to Art History*, Unit 12, Section 4, Erika Langmuir discussed the way the French artist Courbet mixed categories of *genre* and history painting in his painting *The Stonebreakers* (Plate 25). Although *Work* is an allegory, it too can be seen to represent the working man with the heroism and elevated status associated with history painting. The painting went against the grain of a sentimentalized image of the poor that had become prevalent in much Victorian art: it disrupted established artistic canons.

The painting may also be compared with Daniel Maclise's *Peter the Great at Deptford Dockyard* of 1857 (Plate 51). Here labour is represented in the context of a scene from British history – in a seventeenth-century rather than a modern setting. To the left the Tsar is depicted with a saw working at the dockyard; King William III is depicted on the right.

So we are not only dealing with contemporary attitudes towards the working poor but also with how they could be represented in art. In order to make his young, handsome navvy on the left of the composition monumental, Brown has used the type (though not the trappings) of a classical hero. Was this, then, just a simple idealization of the manual worker? Yes, there is a degree of idealization in the picture, but there is another side to the coin. That is, to see the worker as worthy of such elevated treatment was itself a radical gesture. You may recall that Brown wrote of the navvy that 'he was at least as worthy of the powers of an English painter, as the fisherman of the Adriatic, the peasant of the Campagna, or the Neapolitan lazzarone [beggar]'. He saw the worker as a hero of modern life who should not be precluded from the higher canons of art. And the audience was asked to admire and respect manual labour as much as intellectual work.

Brown adapted past traditions, then, to work out a new iconography that could adequately represent modern life. *Work* was the product of choices and decisions over a considerable period. The navvies were part of his conception from the start, though other figures were adapted and changed (see Plate 50). Some changes were suggested by Thomas Plint, the man who commissioned the painting on the basis of the sketch and partial completion of the background in 1856. Plint wrote to the artist, asking:

> Could you introduce *both* Carlyle and Kingsley, and change one of the four *fashionable young* ladies into a *quiet, earnest holy*-looking one, with a book or two and *tracts*? I want *this* point in, for I am much interested in *this* work myself, and know those who are. (Cited in Hueffer, *Ford Madox Brown: a Record of his Life and Work*, p. 112)

Plint's evangelical passion for tracts is acknowledged in the final work, and although Charles Kingsley is not portrayed, the Rev. F. D. Maurice, founder of the Christian Socialist movement (see Section 5.3 below), is shown beside Carlyle – both figures standing *for* intellectual work. Posters for the Working Men's College (at which Brown taught) are also depicted on the wall on the left of the painting.

Plint actually died before *Work* was completed, but on one level the painting was clearly addressed to him. There was a common ground of understanding between the artist and patron – a point you should also bear in mind when you watch television programme 22 on the northern industrialist Leathart, who commissioned a replica of *Work* from Brown. And on a broader level, the image of the poor in *Work* was addressed to a middle-class art public, familiar with the work of Carlyle and ideas of reform. This is an important point in relation to question (2) in Section 1 on the working poor: 'To what extent were they invited to think of themselves in terms of the same values as others?' In the context of Victorian society, and the place of art within it, the lower classes were the objects of art, not its audience.

It does not follow from this, however, that the painting can be reduced to a reflection of the ideology of what may be identified as the dominant classes. It is fair to say, I think, that, like Dickens, Brown does not try to undermine the basic social and economic structure of Victorian society. Instead he questions the kinds of prevailing attitudes and conditions which downgraded the working poor within that system. We have talked about the picture in the context of ideas of reform which were very different from those of Palmerston that you considered at the beginning of these units (Section 3.4 will discuss these competing ideologies).

To consider the ideological framework in which *Work* was produced is to do more than to describe the intellectual ideas deliberately espoused by the artist. The purpose of identifying that broader framework is to account, in some measure, for how those ideas came to be held: it is to look at the beliefs and assumptions underlying them. And in our discussion of *Work* we have looked at one set of beliefs about work and reform that could be shared by Brown and members of his audience.

To think about the kind of 'common consent' which enables members of a social group to see the world in a certain shared way seems to me a useful way of approaching a study of works of art. It avoids seeing the artist as an isolated unit. But it does involve making a distinction – between conscious and explicit ideas (particularly evident in works of art that aim at social comment) and an implicit and covert ideology (as in a shared set of beliefs and assumptions) to which all art must to some extent be subject, whether or not it has an identifiable 'message'.

Explicitly, *Work* can be seen as a type of Carlylean tract, with a Christian message of communion between Carlyle's 'heroes' (workers) and 'healers' (reformers). This is reinforced through the use of biblical quotations on the frame of the painting such as 'in the sweat of thy face shalt thou eat bread' and 'seest thou a man diligent in his business? He shall stand before Kings'. *Work* was didactic – a painting with a message of moral improvement – and an assertion of the dignity of labour.

Implicitly, Brown's treatment of his subject depends on a set of beliefs which enabled work to be seen as *sacred*. If attitudes changed so that the work of the labouring classes became rightfully respected, then society could become a more just place while retaining its basic structure. And to paint *Work* as a Carlylean tract assumed a particular attitude towards the role of the artist. His role was seen to be that of a radical reformer – as part of a responsible élite.

Furthermore, Brown's choice of the navvy as the hero of *Work* provides an example of these explicit and implicit levels of meaning. You may remember from the account you read earlier that Brown said that he chose the navvy as his subject because he saw the 'excavators' at work near his home every day. But that does not explain *why* he considered the navvy appropriate as the central vehicle for his ambitious allegory. His selection and treatment of the navvy was informed by his particular social and intellectual position. The navvy was not a member, after all, of a permanently-based urban proletariat. As a labour force, navvies travelled the country working in teams – and here they are depicted in suburban Hampstead. There is no doubt that navvies were an important part of the labour force at this time – building the railways or, as here, working on the sewerage system. But there is a sense in which Brown's celebration of physical prowess and manual labour to express the idea of work could be seen as rather anachronistic at a time of increasing mechanization. Indeed, it has been suggested that *Work* was a celebration of a particular type of independent manual work that the middle classes could admire.

Does it follow, then, that *Work* represents what reforming spirits within the middle classes *wanted* to believe about the working classes – and about their own relationship to them? Well, if you turn to the words of the navvy interviewed by Henry Mayhew (Supplementary Texts) you will get a very different impression of a navvy's life from that suggested by Brown. Here we encounter the exploitative practices of contractors and conditions which, it is fair to say, Brown knew little about. On this basis, it might be argued that the picture did not represent real conditions. But remember that pictures are not just passive reflections of 'life as lived' – the point I made at the very beginning of this discussion. Moreover, in his allegory of work, Brown was concerned with what relations *should* be like.

If we *simply* match 'art' against 'reality', we are in danger of forgetting, I think, how meanings are produced in art within a tradition of representation; for Brown's painting questioned the 'normal' heroes of art and drew attention to relations between different strata of society. So how the working poor were represented in art was not only limited by prevailing social attitudes but also by artistic possibilities and constraints. If manual labour was idealized in *Work*, the picture went against the grain of what was believed to be an appropriate subject for heroism in art.

3.3 EVANGELICALISM, POVERTY AND RESPECTABILITY

You have already encountered Samuel Smiles and his arguments in favour of independence and self-help – Geoffrey Best actually describes the mid-Victorian belief in these values as a '*cult and sanctification* of self-help and independence' (Best, p. 281).

This emphasis on the virtues and value of individualism, individual effort, initiative, responsibility and hard work *could* be based on purely secular foundations. However, they also coincided with beliefs and attitudes which were central to evangelicalism. In Units 18–19 it was argued that evangelicalism was a major influence on Victorian culture especially in its 'call to seriousness', and its emphasis on duty and responsibility, even when its specifically religious aspect was rejected. The strength of evangelical influence on Victorian culture makes the evangelical view of social morality all the more important.

Religiously, evangelicalism was highly individualist: the sinful individual must recognize his or her own lost condition and personally accept the salvation offered by God, experiencing this conversion by a change of both heart and character. In the social sphere this individualism emerged in a characteristic emphasis, among evangelicals, upon individual effort. In the alleviation and overcoming of poverty and deprivation, for example, evangelicals emphasized the need for hard work and individual effort from the poor themselves and the need for individual charity and work on behalf of the poor from those who were better off. Such hard work and individual effort on the part of the poor themselves also constituted the means of their achieving a measure of respectability. Poor they might be, but if hard working and thus independent of charity, they might also be respectable.

The evangelical message *to* the poor was therefore a clear one: the causes of poverty were too often rooted in personal moral weakness, in lack of effort, idleness, lack of thrift or in drunkenness. The extremely **popular Baptist preacher** C. H. Spurgeon, for example, published two series of tracts giving practical advice. In *John Ploughman's Talk* (1869) and *John Ploughman's Pictures* (1880) Spurgeon urged the poor to see that individual self-help was the key to the improvement of their condition, especially the cultivation of sobriety, hard work, persistence and will power.

However, the evangelical call to the middle classes also embodied a call to social concern. The experience of conversion included the call to duty and to caring for the poor and destitute. The characteristic Victorian evangelical expression of this concern for the poor was charity and philanthropy, and, most especially, the setting up of voluntary societies for the organization and administration of such charitable and philanthropic work. Along with a pervasive sense of seriousness, the evangelical legacy to Victorian society included the highly characteristic Victorian institution – the voluntary society. In 1885, at the funeral of Lord Shaftesbury, who had been the principal leader of the evangelicals in public life from the 1830s, there were representatives of nearly 500 such societies, most of them established during his lifetime and inspired in whole or part by evangelical founders. Even in their charity, however, evangelicals were concerned not to erode the incentive to the poor to work for themselves and thus achieve a respectability which they would otherwise lack. In this, evangelicalism both shared in and contributed to prevailing secular assumptions. The revision of the Poor Law in 1834, the effects of which were felt throughout the period of our case study, sought to make the conditions under which public relief of poverty would be given less desirable than the conditions experienced by the poor not in receipt of public aid. The Charity Organisation Society, set up in 1869 to coordinate the efforts of voluntary philanthropic groups, sought to embody the same principle: charity must not be such as to discourage individuals from working for themselves.

Behind both evangelical charity and evangelical advice to the poor on how to remedy their situation for themselves there lay a common emphasis on the virtue of work. For the middle and upper classes, meanwhile, evangelical charity and philanthropy was not merely a matter of giving one's goods or time; it was also about the serious, useful, responsible use of life, about the completion of a useful life's work. For the poor, work and responsible, thrifty, sober habits were, in evangelical eyes, both the best way to alleviate poverty and the safest way to avoid the sins of laziness, idleness, drunkenness and extravagance. You may recall here the way in which Horace Mann observed that it was the urban working classes who most needed the constraints and consolations of religion yet who most lacked them. In Units 22–26 we shall look more closely at Mann's own view of the relationship between religion and the values and behaviour of the working classes. For the present it is worth reflecting on Mann's comment and comparing it with what Geoffrey Best says in the second paragraph on p. 288 of *Mid-Victorian Britain 1851–75*. Middle-class respectability, Best points out, could include an agnostic choice to stay apart from organized religion, but the desirability of the masses remaining religious, in order to promote social order, was seldom doubted.

We have concentrated on evangelicalism because, either in its straightforwardly religious form or in its diffused effects in Victorian society, it exercised so great and characteristic an influence on Victorian attitudes to poverty, to work and to ideas of respectability. It stressed work as the primary source of the escape from poverty and the main source of respectability, even within a poor standard of living; it praised individual effort and initiative; it favoured private, voluntary and charitable means of relieving poverty, rather than state intervention and legislation; and saw poverty and its eradication as a matter of individual responsibility . Because poverty was not seen as an effect of environment or social circumstance, middle and upper-class Victorian evangelicalism did not advocate change in social structure. Indeed, Victorian evangelicalism frequently stressed not only individual responsibility *for* poverty but also encouraged a humble acceptance *of* poverty and of a social order in which a hierarchy of rich and poor was held to be divinely ordained. This particular strand of evangelicalism was given classic expression in a verse of the popular hymn 'All things bright and beautiful', written in 1849 by Mrs C. F. Alexander, the wife of the Archbishop of Dublin:

The rich man in his castle
The poor man at his gate
God made them high and lowly
And ordered their estate.

That particular verse is probably one of the most frequently quoted verses of any Victorian hymn, but it is only the most well-known example of a widespread evangelical insistence that acceptance of the social order, and the deference that went with it, was a part of the Christian moral order. However, as we have seen, the expression of such social division between rich and poor within Christianity was also identified by commentators such as Edward Miall as one of the main reasons for working-class alienation from the churches – a point to which we shall return in Units 23–24.

For all its influence, however, evangelicalism was by no means the only religious response to poverty, nor was it, in itself, always as straightforward as the outline above would imply.

Exercise

Read the extract from a sermon preached by the Anglican High Churchman H. P. Liddon in 1876 which you will find in the Course Reader (extract III. 8), and consider how far Liddon discusses the question of poverty and work in terms which differ from the characteristic evangelical one outlined above.

Discussion

There is no simple answer to this exercise. Liddon does not *explicitly* contradict the view of poverty and work which evangelicalism characteristically put forward. I suggest, however, that his overall tone is less austere, less severe, and more aware of the ambiguities surrounding the problem of poverty and the nature of work. Work, he recognizes, can often be a burden – mechanical, oppressive and restrictive of any finer feeling. He also acknowledges that the poor may not have the kind of work which enables them to gain independence. He also gives more weight to the influence of society and environment in shaping the circumstances of working-class life: civilization, he says, has often made the poor man what he is and this poverty may itself destroy self-respect rather than pose a challenge to be met with hard work and self-help. Finally, he advocates a combination of 'wise philanthropy' *and* 'wise laws' – concerning holidays, hours of work, housing conditions and education – as a remedy for the problem of poverty.

Evangelicalism itself was also aware of the ambiguities to which Liddon draws attention. Although representatives of the evangelical tradition such as Spurgeon continued to proclaim a particularly clear version of their social values throughout the period of our case study, other evangelicals, before and after 1850, recognized the need for state action and legislation as well as philanthropy and hard work. Thus evangelicals frequently campaigned for reforms in factory conditions, housing conditions and in a host of other areas, as well as campaigning for state action in respect of moral issues such as drinking, gambling, sabbath observance, child care and prostitution.

By the time of Liddon's sermon in 1876 there were other important strands to Victorian Christian social thought. In the late 1840s and early 1850s a group of Anglicans led by F. D. Maurice (who is portrayed in Ford Madox Brown's *Work*), J. M. Ludlow and Thomas Hughes called for the development of a Christian Socialism in which the church would take up the cause of the poor and the working classes. Although it failed at that time to establish a firm basis within the church, the movement made significant contributions to Victorian working-class life and organization through its work in the early cooperative movement and the founding of the Working Men's College. It also influenced a later generation of Anglicans in the 1870s and '80s who formed more enduring groups within the Church of England to campaign on a Christian Socialist platform.

These later groupings, such as the Guild of St Matthew and the Christian Social Union, advocated much greater state intervention and legislation to overcome poverty and social deprivation, and saw the problems of the poor more in terms of the pressure of environment, circumstance and social conditions, and less in terms of individual effort, responsibility or personal and moral failing.

Nonconformists also developed their own version of a 'social gospel' in the later Victorian period. Among the more working-class Nonconformists there was often considerable overlap between membership and leadership in chapel and trade-union life. Primitive Methodism especially was prominent in the development of, for example, the Durham Miners Union and the Agricultural Workers Union. Middle-class Nonconformists, meanwhile, developed ideas such as the 'civic gospel' combining Christian social concern with municipal welfare and the reform of the urban environment. In radio programme 15, later in the course, we shall examine the contribution of one particular Nonconformist, the Congregationalist minister R. W. Dale, to the development of the 'civic gospel' in Victorian Birmingham.

These developments reflected both changing secular attitudes and changing theological emphases. From a secular standpoint, churchmen, along with other Victorian leaders, were forced by sheer weight of evidence to recognize that voluntary, charitable provision, whether in housing, education, poor relief or whatever, just was not enough. The problems posed by urban, industrial society were too great and too complex for such piecemeal palliatives; they required government initiatives and resources: secular as well as religious observers came to see the need for 'wise philanthropy *and* wise laws'.

These developments, however, also had a theological dimension. The evangelical emphasis on the doctrine of the atonement – the idea that the sacrificial death of Christ saved sinful men and women from the wrathful judgement of God – had been central to much of early Victorian Christianity. Increasingly, however, that doctrine came under pressure as morally dubious and founded on an uncritical reading of the Bible: the authors of *Essays and Reviews*, for example, criticized the evangelical view of atonement on these grounds. Mid and late Victorian Christianity tended to lay greater emphasis on the moral teaching of the prophets, on the life of Jesus and his role as an ethical teacher, and upon the Fatherhood rather than the judgement of God, and hence also on the brotherhood of man. This theological change, together with the sheer pressure of urban poverty, prompted a steady increase in calls from religious leaders for a combination of 'wise laws' and 'wise philanthropy' and a softening of the more severe and austere evangelical line.

3.4 THE GOSPEL OF WORK

You have seen that both Dickens and Brown offered a tribute to Thomas Carlyle – Dickens by inscribing *Hard Times* to him and Brown by including Carlyle in his painting *Work*. Although Carlyle lived till 1881, his most influential books were written in the 1830s and '40s. You read about some of Carlyle's writings in Units 13–15, Part I. Carlyle was seen by many as the foremost social critic of his day. His influence may have waned somewhat by the mid-Victorian period, but his ideas continued to be taken up, not only by Dickens but later by writers such as William Morris.

One influential aspect of Carlyle's thought which is perhaps less prominent in Dickens but is to the fore in Brown's painting concerns the value of work. The Victorians almost universally praised hard work. But it is important to notice that their reasons for doing so were not always the same. Smiles and Palmerston, whom we have been presenting to you as spokesmen for the 'dominant ideology', praised hard work, but they praised it as a form of self-help, as a means of advancing to a respectable independence. And they stressed it in relation to working-class men in the context of the idea of 'removable inequalities'. To repeat Palmerston's words: '... depend upon it, you will, *by systematic industry*, raise yourselves in the social system of this country' (Best, p. 258).

Carlyle, however, regarded hard work as bringing, so to speak, its own rewards, as something to be valued in itself, even as possessing a kind of religious value. More than anyone else he is regarded as the prophet of what came to be called 'the Gospel of Work'. I think you will see from the following extract why Carlyle should be so regarded:

> There is a perennial nobleness, and even sacredness, in Work. Were he never so benighted, forgetful of his high calling, there is always hope in a man that actually and earnestly works: in Idleness alone is there perpetual despair. Work, never so Mammonish, mean, *is* in communication with Nature; the real desire to get Work done will itself lead one more and more to truth, to Nature's appointments and regulations which are truth.
>
> The latest Gospel in this world is, Know thy work and do it. 'Know thyself': long enough has that poor 'self' of thine tormented thee; thou wilt never get to 'know' it, I believe! Think it not thy business, this of knowing thyself; thou art an unknowable individual: know what thou canst work at; and work at it, like a Hercules! That will be thy better plan.
>
> It has been written, 'an endless significance lies in Work'; a man perfects himself by working. Foul jungles are cleared away, fair seed-fields rise instead, and stately cities; and withal the man himself first ceases to be a jungle and foul unwholesome desert thereby. Consider how, even in the meanest sorts of Labour, the whole soul of a man is composed into a kind of real harmony, the instant he sets himself to work! Doubt, Desire, Sorrow, Remorse, Indignation, Despair itself, all these like helldogs lie beleaguering the soul of the poor dayworker, as of every man: but he bends himself with free valour against his task, and all these are stilled, all these shrink murmuring far off into their caves. The man is now a man. The blessed glow of Labour in him, is it not a purifying fire, wherein all poison is burnt up, and of sour smoke itself there is made bright blessed flame! (Carlyle, *Past and Present*, Book III, Chapter 11)

It is evident from these remarks that Carlyle was a religious man, though not in a conventional way. His background was in the Protestant tradition in which the 'work ethic' had long been fostered. It is interesting to note that the support of the Protestant traditions, including that of evangelicalism, was found both for the instrumental view of work implied by the ideology claimed to be the 'dominant' one and for the 'Gospel of Work'. Indeed, there would be no inconsistency in regarding work in both ways. But 'the Gospel of Work' as expounded by Carlyle can readily give rise to the expectation that work should be satisfying and developed into a critique of the repetitious and monotonous kind of work which was to be found in factories. It thus contains the seeds of ideological divergence such as we find in the writings of William Morris (see Section 5.4 below). Ideological competition was by no means as absent from mid-Victorian Britain as Best implies. It is true that neither Carlyle nor Dickens was calling in question the social hierarchy. But their ideas are by no means the same as those who accepted what Best refers to as 'the social theory of removable inequalities' (see Section 2.2 above). It might be truer to say, not that there was a consensus or that there was a single 'dominant' ideology but that where there was a conflict of ideas and values it had implications for the social order which stopped well short of being revolutionary.

4 ROLES AND REPRESENTATIONS OF WOMEN

A striking fact about what has been claimed to be the 'dominant ideology' of mid-Victorian Britain is that it makes no mention of women. A man could only be 'respectable', as we have seen, if he was able to fend for himself. For most men this requirement put a premium on self-help and hard work. Hard physical labour, as idealized in Ford Madox Brown's *Work*, acquired a dignity it did not have before. And there was even some tendency to disapprove of the idle rich – not for being rich but for being 'idle'. But though many working-class women worked, and worked hard, there was little idealization of them. What the Victorians expected of a reasonable woman was not only different from what they expected of a reasonable man, it was in some respects quite the opposite. It was entirely respectable for a woman to be a dependent for her whole life and only in certain circumstances could a woman be independent without compromising her respectability. The reason for this has to do with what was perceived as the special place of the woman at home.

4.1 A CONVENTIONAL VIEW OF THE ROLE OF WOMEN

Best has a few pages on the mid-Victorian home, which you should read now: from the middle of p. 300 to p. 305. Compare what Best has to say with the following short passage from Samuel Smiles's *Life and Labour* (1887):

> There cannot be a doubt that Christian civilisation has greatly elevated the position of woman, and enabled her to preserve that manhood of the soul which acknowledges no sex. It is through her influence that men and women are taught these divine lessons of morality and religion which maintain the reign of civilisation. It is at the sanctuary of the domestic hearth that woman rules the world as much as if she herself possessed the reins of government (pp. 386ff.)

Exercise

I'd like you to make some notes on the points at which you think the passage from Smiles's book gives supporting evidence for what Best has to say and where it seems to give evidence in another direction.

Specimen answer

1 Women, according to Best, were consigned to a subordinate, domestic role (pp. 301ff.) though their position was becoming 'less unenviable' towards the end of the mid-Victorian period. Smiles, writing (it should be noted) in a rather later period, pays lip service to the idea of a fundamental equality between men and women and yet clearly assigns to women a primarily domestic role and, insofar as their authority is limited to the home, a clearly subordinate one.

2 Both acknowledge the special role of women in teaching morality and religion and indeed the importance of this teaching for society. Best writes that 'the Victorians... proclaimed the Christian home as at once the finest source of human virtue and the firmest foundation-stone of social order' (p. 300). Morality and piety were best inculcated 'at mother's knee'. Smiles's account confirms this – it is mother who teaches 'these divine lessons of morality and religion which maintain the reign of civilisation'.

Discussion

The idealization of home life is part and parcel of an idealization of women, as if, according to this view, they were specially gifted in matters of morality and religion. This has two implications for the Victorian perception of women. One is that sexual immorality was seen as a much more serious failing in a woman than it was in a man – the infamous 'double standard'. The other is that, insofar as women were involved in work outside the home, there were certain types of work which it was especially appropriate for them to do, for example, work with religious and charitable organizations. The scope for women outside the home was increasing in Britain in the latter half of the nineteenth century. And it is significant that while Smiles in his 1887 *Life and Labour* mostly discusses women in their supportive (to men) role – as what he calls 'help-meets' – he is neither able to ignore nor disapprove of the work of such women as Florence Nightingale (1820–1910). He even supported the higher education of women, though not as a means of changing the place of women in society, but rather as a way of enhancing the fulfilment of their basic domestic role.

You should now listen to cassette 4, side 1, band 2 *Women Artists and Writers* where the role of women as artists and writers is discussed.

4.2 IMAGES OF WOMEN IN PRE-RAPHAELITE PAINTING

How were women represented in art? And how did images of women relate to prevailing attitudes towards the role and nature of women? These are the questions that I shall address in this section by looking at a selection of paintings by the Pre-Raphaelites and by an artist associated with them, Augustus Egg.

In this discussion of images of women, I shall consider one aspect of that framework of attitudes and beliefs: the dichotomy between the 'pure' and the 'fallen', the Madonna and the Magdalen. This opposition was common currency in the period: on the one hand, the virtuous role within the family – seen, for instance, at its crudest and most sentimental, in George Elgar Hicks's series of pictures called *Woman's Mission* (1863) comprising *Companion of Manhood* (Plate 55), *Guide of Childhood* and *Comfort of Old Age* – on the other hand, domesticity was disturbed and family relationships broken in Richard Redgrave's picture of the erring daughter in *The Outcast* (1851, Plate 57). The opposition was certainly not always black and white, but was an essential part of the framework within which representations of women were produced.

Rossetti stressed that his early work *The Girlhood of Mary Virgin* (1848–9, Plate 56) 'was a symbol of female excellence. The Virgin being taken as its highest type'. He used his sister Christina as his model for the Virgin – as he did again for *Ecce Ancilla Domini!* ('Behold the handmaiden of the Lord!', Plate 41) – rather than employ the trite, ideal female types favoured by the academic artist Eastlake (discussed in Units 18–19, Section 6). Both these pictures were as much concerned with the contemporary woman *as* Virgin and *as* Madonna, as they were with representing Mary as a contemporary type. For these are motifs of an ideal female purity and innocence, which reappear in contemporary genre scenes and, as you will see later, in the literature of the period.

The woman's role as guardian of the home, the private sphere, was seen as central not only to family life, but to the orderly conduct of social life in general. In Holman Hunt's *The Children's Holiday (Portrait of Mrs Thomas Fairbairn and her children)* (1864–5, Plate 60) the woman is represented as mother and protector of children, and indeed as the wife of the wealthy Thomas Fairbairn who commissioned the picture. They are depicted in the park of their country house; social status is also signified through details of jewellery and dress; the tea service depicted – with its impressive array of silver – suggests both family ritual and the conspicuous display of affluence. As a patron of the Pre-Raphaelites, Fairbairn had already bought Holman Hunt's *The Awakening Conscience* (1854, Colour Plate 18) – a picture with a subject which contrasts with that ideal of womanhood and Victorian domesticity.

In Unit 17 you were asked to think about Hunt's religious and moral concerns in *The Light of the World* (Colour Plate 17) and *The Awakening Conscience*. I am sure you found some elements of the pictures more easily 'readable' than others. And you should not worry if you found the subject of *The Awakening Conscience* particularly hard to work out. This difficulty may tell us something about the distance between Victorian culture and our own. To understand what the picture meant in Victorian terms, we need to consider the 'story' on which it relies so heavily for its meaning.

Exercise

So now look again at Colour Plate 18 and read Ruskin's letter to *The Times* (Course Reader, extract III.4). As you do so, identify the 'story' of the work. How does Ruskin relate the interior depicted to the idea of home?

Discussion

She, as the kept mistress, represents the fallen woman and he, her seducer. Telling details – such as the lack of a ring on her wedding finger – signify the nature of their relationship. It is the moment of her recognition of her past sins, precipitated by the words of 'oft in the stilly night'. Ruskin comments on the 'fatal newness; nothing there that has the old thoughts of home upon it, or that is ever to become part of home'. The interior depicted in the painting undermines the ideal of home as a haven of stability and virtuous domesticity.

The painting represents a contemporary social theme imbued with moral and religious significance. But the whole meaning of the work does depend on being 'rightly read', in Ruskin's words. A pre-occupation with a didactic, story-telling art was linked with Victorian tastes in literature and the novel as a literary form. But the painter works with the two-dimensional surface of the canvas and his or her narrative has to depend on different skills and devices from those used by the writer. Gombrich has made the point that 'There must be a great difference between a painting that illustrates a known story and another that wishes to *tell* a story' (*Action and Expression in Western Art*). And in the 1850s, Ruskin had welcomed the idea of artists 'becoming poets themselves in the entire sense, and inventing the story as they painted it' (Ruskin, *Modern Painters*, Vol. 3, p. 97). *The Awakening Conscience* is clearly an attempt to tell a story, and to tell a story with a moral message. This may be compared with Rossetti's *Ecce Ancilla Domini!*, an Annunciation, a known story. But *The Awakening Conscience* did represent a story known in the wider sense, in terms of contemporary social life. In these terms, an artist never makes a story out of nothing, but out of the material at his or her disposal – that is, the available currency of ideas, attitudes and beliefs, and the specific skills and conventions of art. So let us now look at Hunt's 'material' in this broad sense and how he handles it.

Like the other Pre-Raphaelites, Hunt initially saw himself as 'Bohemian', somehow apart from bourgeois society and its conventions, despite the Pre-Raphaelites' middle-class origins and their dependence on a middle-class audience. Annie Miller was the working-class model who posed for the figure of the woman in *The Awakening Conscience*. She was one of several working-class women to enter the circle – women who began as models and became mistresses, and eventually wives too in the cases of Elizabeth Siddal and Jane Burden. With something of the missionary zeal mentioned in Units 18–19, Hunt set himself up as her guardian and hoped to marry her once she had been 'improved'. Miller seems to have resisted the kind of transformation he envisaged and eventually rejected him. On one level Hunt's own experience informed the work but not in a straightforward sense, for this is not the personal story of Hunt and Miller.

The Awakening Conscience deals with both relations between men and women and between classes. So the work was informed by the broader social significance of the 'fallen woman', manifested in the public concern with the issue of sexual morality. The idea of the 'conscience' that may or may not be 'awakened' suggests a conflict within women between the states of innocence and sin. This was vividly represented in the stereotypical polarity between the Madonna and

Magdalen in Hunt's *Christ and the Two Marys*, (1847, Plate 61). Hunt envisaged *The Awakening Conscience* and *The Light of the World* as a pair. It was in the pathos of Dickens's description of Peggotty's search for little Emily in *David Copperfield* that Hunt saw the possibility of the theme of the fallen woman and her redemption as the 'material embodiment' of *The Light of the World*. It was the 'Repentent Magdalen' motif updated. Its identity as a modern parable was reinforced by the accompanying quotations from the scriptures which appeared on the frame and in the catalogue of the 1854 Royal Academy Show. In the picture, the idea of repentance is signified largely through the use of the mirror as a narrative device. The mirror reflects the garden (i.e. innocence) which she is looking towards for salvation.

Ruskin stressed the symbolic function of the interior, its vulgarity, and its 'fatal newness'. To Ruskin, taste was the external expression of moral value and modern furniture spelt a *nouveau riche* mentality: the attributes of gentility were acquired but served only as trappings. Note, for example, the new piano and the unread books. Though the decor depicted was seen as vulgar, the painting was not, for Ruskin stressed 'There is never vulgarity in a *whole* truth however commonplace' (Ruskin, *Modern Painters*, Vol. 3, p. 90). And the 'whole truth' was expressed in the redemptive theme of the painting. The theme was apparent in the work as seen by Ruskin, but subsequently emphasized in Hunt's reworking of the woman's face at Fairbairn's request: he had found the 'ghastly' expression disturbing and wished to emphasize her potential salvation.

I have suggested how Hunt's picture was produced in terms of prevailing ideas about women and class. But how and what a picture represents also relates to the artistic traditions on which it depends. It was the eighteenth century artist Hogarth on whom Victorian painters drew heavily for their narrative style and didactic content (see Hogarth's *Before* and *After*, 1736, Plates 58 and 59). The contemporary audience was familiar with the artistic representation of repentance; in the established 'awakened conscience' subject Hunt modified and adapted this though retaining the idea of a return to moral convention. The important point about *The Awakening Conscience* is that Hunt applied the morally acceptable theme of repentance to the problematic subject of the 'fallen woman'.

The Needlewoman at Home and Abroad.

AT HOME.   ABROAD.

Figure 4 Punch *cartoon, 'The Needlewoman at Home and Abroad', 1850. Emigration was seen as one of the solutions to the growing problem of prostitution. (Photo:* Punch, *volume 18, page 15)*

The lives of 'fallen women' were recorded in the *Morning Chronicle* in Henry Mayhew's famous letters on prostitution amongst seamstresses. Mayhew saw this as an urgent social problem and identified poverty as its main cause. The exploitation of needleworkers had been Redgrave's subject in *The Seamstress* (Plate 62) exhibited at the Royal Academy in 1846. And Millais's drawing *Virtue and Vice* (1853, Plate 63) is directly linked to the plight of the needlewoman, here shown tempted by prostitution. As the Punch cartoon (Figure 4) indicates, this was topical social issue. It was a widespread belief that neglect of conventional sexual morality was a threat to the social order. Commentators such as William Acton, for instance, saw prostitution as a moral outrage caused primarily be the inherent corruption of women themselves; other commentators places more stress on the idea of the woman as victim.

Rossetti's *Found* (1854–82) (Colour Plate 31) also engaged with the contemporary social issue of prostitution, but it was never completed. A drawing by Rossetti (Figure 5) shows us the complete composition envisaged. The scene is set against the background of Blackfriars bridge, extending towards the countryside. The drover is depicted meeting the woman to whom he was once betrothed, now 'fallen'. And she is shown *literally* fallen to the ground at the

Figure 5   Rossetti Finished drawing for Found, *pen and brown ink and some indian ink and grey wash, 20.6 × 18.75cm. Signed and dated 1853. (Photo: Trustees of the British Museum)*

recognition of her past life, a motif with well-established precedents including George Morland's *The Fair Penitent* (1789, Plate 64). One of the problems identified by contemporary social commentators was the influx of poor country girls into the city. Unable to earn enough money, they turned to prostitution. In *Found,* the darkness of the woman's shawl is contrasted with the whiteness (purity) of the drover's smock: the idea of the innocence of the country is thus compared with the depravity of the city. So, in order to retrieve meaning in the work we need to recognize its dependence on social attitudes and reformist causes.

Both Rossetti and Hunt had searched hard for typical cases, indicative of contemporary concerns with the 'empirical survey'. For example, Mayhew had sought the typical and the representative, saying 'I seek no extreme cases'. But whereas Mayhew had warned against the dangers of middle-class philanthropy, Hunt and Rossetti saw themselves as arbiters of social, moral and spiritual values. Their treatments reinforced conventional notions of social morality. A concern with redemption to some extent sanctioned a strong element of voyeurism. It also sanctioned the treatment of a problematic subject – for prostitution and female adultery threatened established social convention, evoking fears of the dislocation of ordered social life.

Finally, I want you to look at a set of three pictures – or triptych – painted by Augustus Egg (1858, Colour Plate 32), now known as *Past and Present,* although it was initially untitled. When exhibited at the Royal Academy, the group of three paintings was accompanied by the following quotation:

> August the 4th. Have just heard that B ... has been dead more than a fortnight, so his poor children have now lost both their parents. I hear *she* was seen on Friday last near the Strand, evidently without a place to lay her head. What a fall hers has been!

In the central painting in the narrative series, the adulterous woman is depicted pleading with her husband in a middle-class interior. Beside her is the rotten apple, symbolic of her fall. The woman's fate is depicted on the left as she huddles with her illegitimate child under the arches near the Thames. On the right, the daughters are shown in moonlight praying for their lost mother. A moral contrast is thereby drawn between corruption and innocence. The pictures depict the destruction of Victorian home and family. It has been argued that the triptych was an explicit commentary on the divorce law, the Matrimonial Causes Act of 1857 (which Best discusses, you may remember, on p. 303). With this act, divorce became accessible to the middle classes. Previously an act of parliament had been required and therefore divorce had only been available to the very wealthy. Egg's attitude towards the woman is debatable but it is certainly no endorsement of her moral position. It rather encapsulates those fears and anxieties felt by many that with the ease of divorce, moral bankruptcy would quickly result in the breakdown of the home.

But as *art,* the representation of contemporary moral and social life was subject to public expectations of what art should be like. *The Athenaeum* (1 May, 1858) objected:

> Mr Egg's unnamed picture is divided into three compartments, each more ghastly and terrible than the other, till in the last we come to such a sink of misery and loathsomeness, painted with such an unhealthy determination to dissect horror and to catalogue the dissecting room that we turn from what is a real and possible terror as from an impure thing that seems out of place in a gallery of laughing brightness, where young, unstained, unpainted and happy faces come to chat and trifle. There must be a line drawn as to where the horrors that should not be painted for public and innocent sight begin, and we think Mr Egg has put one foot at least beyond this line.

Exercise

In what ways did the reviewer think Egg had gone too far?

Discussion

Several points were raised by the reviewer – such as the possible corruptive power of knowledge on the innocent. But the most significant comment, I think, is the line to be drawn, in terms of appropriateness of subject matter. It was clearly considered that Egg had gone too far: though he depicts the social and moral consequences, he did not add the redemptive angle to the story as others had done.

Furthermore, a painting with adultery as its central theme was on public display, and the Academy was a popular venue for Society. Also, Egg's accompanying quotation *seemed* to come from a diary – that is, anonymous, but apparently true. This *suggested* a piece of social documentation rather than a religious tract. But whereas this was appropriate to social investigators such as Mayhew, or moral commentators such as Acton, in a series of paintings this was seen to have broken with an artistic decorum, with what was a proper subject matter for art.

In this section, we have considered how meanings in art were produced within an ideological framework, characterized by an opposition between the 'pure' and the 'fallen' woman, the Madonna and the Magdalen. In the pictures we have looked at, we have seen how these classifications were mutually dependent – the one defining the other – as two sides of the same coin. The framework can be seen as 'ideological' in that roles that are social in character are ascribed to women as the essential and *natural* characteristics of the female sex. Ruskin's timeless ideal of womanhood which is discussed in the next section can also be seen as an example of the way certain types of social behaviour were deemed absolute and unchanging.

4.3 THE PLACE OF WOMEN: REPRESENTATIONS OF THE IDEAL IN LITERATURE

In literature as in visual art there is evidence of the different ways Victorians valued women's role in their society. In the following pages we shall look first at an example of an idealized view of woman and ask how it invited women to see themselves as fulfilling a role essentially different from that of men. We shall look then at two other extracts and ask how they illuminate some of the problems inherent in the ideal view of women. The first extract is from John Ruskin's 'Of Queens' Gardens', one of two lectures on the roles of men and women, together entitled *Sesame and Lilies*, which he delivered to a largely middle-class audience in Manchester Town Hall in 1864. The lectures were published in book form in 1865 and proved to be one of Ruskin's most popular works.

Exercise

Read extract III. 7 in the Course Reader now, as far as 'and lighted fire in' at the end of the second paragraph. When you finish, note down the contrasts he uses to define male and female roles.

Discussion

Ruskin differentiates both the qualities and functions of men and women: man's place is with the 'rough work of the open world' and woman's is in the home, where she is 'protected from all danger and temptation'. Where man's power is active, progressive and defensive, woman's is for 'rule'; where his intellect is for 'speculation and invention', hers is for 'sweet ordering, arrangement and decision'. Where his energy is 'for adventure, for war and for conquest', 'her great function is Praise'. When in the course of his duty man 'must be wounded, or subdued, often misled, and *always* hardened', woman is 'guarded from all this', yet nevertheless 'infallibly adjudges the crown of conquest'.

Exercise

What basic assumptions do these definitions make about the roles of men and women?

Discussion

For a twentieth-century reader perhaps the most obvious assumption of Ruskin's definitions is the clear and absolute division between men and women as regards their nature, power and function. It assumes separate and essentially different spheres for the sexes, and places the woman's role exclusively in the private sphere of home and family. Once we recognize this assumption, we also recognize how it must ignore those areas of Victorian society where women had to work in the 'open world', and where they did not, as middle-class woman increasingly could, enjoy the material wealth necessary before exclusively 'separate spheres' could be a reality.

Exercise

Now read paragraph three, beginning 'And wherever a true wife comes', and the following paragraph, taking notes on those qualities Ruskin says women must have to fulfil their role as rulers of the home. Do you find any problems inherent in his assertions?

Discussion

According to Ruskin, woman's role as ruler requires her to be 'incorruptibly good: instinctively, infallibly wise' and 'incapable of error'; qualities which seem actually to lift her out of the realm of the human altogether. By so doing, Ruskin avoids the problem he might otherwise have: to show exactly how women can acquire these perfect virtues. The underlying question he does not address is, if women are to judge the contests of the world, where do they find the wisdom and understanding required if they have no access to or knowledge of that world?

Ruskin does not solve this potential problem directly, but uses the remainder of his lecture to exhort and challenge the women of his audience to extend their idea of the home beyond its physical limits and to spread its moral influence into the outer world.

Exercise

Now read the rest of the extract, and make notes to the following questions:

1 What special qualities does Ruskin attribute to women and how does he assume they can be effective in the world?

2 What criticism does he make of women and their present use of power?

3 What kind of language does Ruskin draw on to persuade women of their duty to the nation?

Discussion

1 He seems to grant women a special place in the world's attentions – 'Queens you must always be' – and a special capacity for moral judgement and sympathy: women must choose the causes for which men fight, and they alone 'can feel the depth of pain and conceive of its healing'. A few pages before this he had prepared his audience to accept that what women are to the home – givers of order, comfort and beauty – they must also be to the nation, 'the woman's duty is to assist in the ordering, in the comforting, in the beautiful adornment of the state'.

2 Ruskin accuses women of being 'too often idle and careless queens', of avoiding the duties incumbent on them: 'you shut yourselves within your park walls'. But even worse, he says, women choose worthless goals rather than moral

and spiritual duties, 'abdicating majesty to play at precedence with their next-door neighbour!'. Ultimately, Ruskin even blames women for the existence of the ills of the world, which they alone, he says, could hinder: 'there is no suffering, no injustice, no misery in the earth, but the guilt lies with you'.

3   In these final pages of his lecture, Ruskin draws on the mediaeval image of woman as the pure Lady, surrounded by her vassals, but with the injunction that *she* must 'see to it' that she serve *them*, the terms of her service being moral and spiritual. Her vassals may serve by feeding and protecting her, but her role is no other than to 'redeem' them, not to lead them 'into captivity'. The last two phrases give a clue to Ruskin's increasing reliance on images and language of the Bible to make his final points. His references to the aesthetic and sensuous pleasures of gardens suggest woman's function as a bringer of joy and beauty, but the religious and moral qualities we associate with Biblical gardens receive the greatest stress. Woman is not meant simply to enjoy her garden, but to give life to its flowers, which Ruskin turns into something more than emblems of beauty and decoration; they become metaphors for the human lives it is woman's duty to save: 'She should revive; the harebells should bloom, not stoop as she passes'. Pressing his message further, Ruskin challenges the 'Queens' of his audience to attend to the 'feeble florets' lying 'in the darkness of the terrible streets'; flowers, he says, 'that have thoughts like yours, and lives like yours; which once saved, you save forever'.

Despite the secular venue of his lectures, Ruskin's message finishes in a frenzy of Biblical references to 'The Song of Solomon', the Garden of Eden, and the Garden of Gethsemane, giving a missionary zeal to his appeal to women to fulfil their role as moral rulers of the nation. The final impression, however, is that the argument is strong in persuasive rhetoric rather than practical advice. What he does not, and perhaps cannot, do is indicate the actual sources of power and where the avenues to it lie. One is left with a sense that women are somehow to fulfil these duties in a world from which, as Ruskin himself stipulates, their experience is largely excluded.

Behind the duty of every woman to be the moral and spiritual 'Queen' of her domestic domain lay the danger represented by the 'feeble florets' and the allusion to Mary Magdalene at the end of *Sesame and Lilies*. That is the danger of the 'Fallen Woman', the reverse side of the coin whose acceptable image was the wife and mother as madonna-like queen, who was, as you have already seen, a compelling subject in Victorian painting. For the purposes of the work that follows we shall confine the idea of the 'fallen woman' to the woman as wife and mother who forsakes the legal bonds of marriage for a liaison which surrenders that respectability defined by the institution of marriage itself. Such a destinction highlights the particularly threatening aspect of this 'fallen woman' to Victorian moral values, centred as they were in the home and family. And it differentiates her from the thousands of women and child prostitutes or unmarried mothers, for whose 'salvation', both physical and spiritual, so many Victorians were deeply concerned and practically engaged. We shall look now at two pieces by women writers which touch on the theme of the 'fallen woman'; in doing so, we can see some of the implications in the idealized view of the Victorian woman which Ruskin's account of her does not allow.

Exercise

Read Elizabeth Barrett Browning's poem 'Lord Walter's Wife' (extract III. 3 in the Course Reader). How does it represent questions about the idealization of womanhood differently from Ruskin? It might help if you focus on the following questions:

1   What marks the difference between the first two verses and verse three?
2   What is the argument put by Lord Walter's wife in verses twelve to sixteen?
3   Does this poem rely on an idealization of womanhood which is comparable to Ruskin's?

Discussion

1 In its first two verses the poem seems to be an idyllic scene like many which would be familiar to a Victorian reader. The beautiful, alluring lady and a lover who fears being caught by her seductive charms was a subject common to many old ballads, and was revived by Romantic poets, such as John Keats in 'La Belle Dame Sans Merci', and used later by Tennyson, too, in the mediaeval settings of much of his popular poetry. But the atmosphere of a past tradition evoked in the first two verses (which could tempt the reader into escaping into a fanciful world) is abruptly broken by a change of language and tone in verse three. Here we are plunged back into the more modern world of colloquial informality, noticeable in the rhythms and subject matter. These two frames of reference, one to an ideal world of chivalry and the other suggesting the real, contemporary Victorian world, provide the framework of oppositions we need to recognize in order to grasp what the poem is doing. Essentially our complacent expectations of a comfortable ballad have been unsettled and we are made to attend fully to the terms of the wife's argument when it comes.

2 The wife accuses her husband's friend of exploiting an idealization of women in order to justify his desire for her and then, when he is thwarted, of exonerating himself by blaming the woman for being 'too fair'. Lord Walter's wife confronts the friend with his own contradiction, asking how she can be 'too fair' to resist (verse two), yet 'no longer fair' (verse ten) when she appears to respond to his advances. She exposes his 'too fair' as a fraudulent means of excusing his own sexual appetite – it is no praise of her virtue at all. The poem thus turns out to be the opposite of what its first two verses suggest: rather than a story of how the beautiful lady sets a trap to seduce her husband's friend, it reveals itself as a trap to catch the friend out at his self-deceiving and offensive game of betraying the husband and blaming the wife.

3 By means of its mocking tone and ironic use of the mediaeval or romantic ballad, the poem discloses the absurdity behind certain popular images of the ideal woman. It humorously attacks as nonsense the male attitude which places woman on a moral pedestal, making her an object of veneration which only hides the fact that she is being treated as an object of gratification. Lord Walter's wife concludes that such an attitude does nothing but disguise an uglier truth: 'You take us for harlots, I tell you, and/not for the women we are' (verse twenty-five).

As a whole the poem appeals to the reader to recognize the contradictory core of such idealizations of women and to see them as masks which hide both the desire and power of men. On the other hand, one can feel that the poem also gives the voice of Lord Walter's wife a certain special weight which does make her the image of an ideal wife. She is never tempted to fall from her pedestal, and the very fact that *she* is the one to see and expose the contradictions in the male attitude gives her the position of moral authority. There is moral superiority in her final words, despite their tone of light mockery to the offended and offending suitor:

> Have I hurt you indeed? We are quits
>   then. Nay, friend of my Walter,
>   be mine!
> Come Dora my darling, my angel, and
>   help me to ask him to dine.

Even though Elizabeth Barrett Browning's sardonic look at the problems of idealizing women contrasts broadly with Ruskin's heavily sermonizing ideal, it nevertheless relies basically on two assumptions which resemble Ruskin's ideal. One is that woman's supreme role is that of the loving wife and mother, and the other, that her supreme virtue is that of unerring moral judgement.

I would like now to turn to another example of the treatment of the 'fallen woman', taken from George Eliot's last novel, *Daniel Deronda*, published in 1876.

Exercise

Read paragraphs two and three beginning from 'It was full ten years', to 'daughter of a noble house' (extract III. 9 in the Course Reader). In the novel, Mrs Glasher is the mistress of the aristocrat, Grandcourt, and mother of his illegitimate children. In this passage, the authorial voice in the novel provides the reader with the history of Mrs Glasher's present situation. What is the predominant tone of the final paragraph? What attitude does it express with regard to Mrs Glasher?

Discussion

The tone is matter-of-fact, almost journalistic, emphasizing how Mrs Glasher exists for the public at large as an absence only occasionally registered in the musing speculation of gossip. It proceeds with a list of observations indirectly portraying the very tone and style of the social class which ostracized Mrs Glasher, yet can still find her and Mr Grandcourt of passing conversational interest: they would make comments such as, it was only 'natural' and 'desirable' that Grandcourt should have 'disentangled' himself from Mrs Glasher, and that he must 'of course' have tired of her, and they would take it for granted that he would eventually 'desire to make a suitable marriage'.

Exercise

How does the final summarizing analogy of the last paragraph provide a different view of the affair, and does this differ from the other extracts we have looked at?

Discussion

It seems to me to suggest a view more critical of public opinion than of the 'fallen woman' herself. The end of the passage no longer employs the tone of urbane sophistication or the language of the social world to which Mrs Glasher and Grandcourt belong. It seems rather to stand apart from that world and expose its values by its critical analogy between the 'lost' and the 'seaworthy' vessels. The double standard by which men and women are judged is neatly encapsulated in the woman's 'fall' being comparable to a vessel lost at sea about whom people eventually lose interest, as though the woman's fate were simply a matter of newsworthiness. On the other hand, the man in the affair need not be hidden from view but may carry on a fully visible, 'seaworthy' life, almost triumphant in his exploits, 'his colours flying'. We register the novelist's condemnation of this double standard in the association we are asked to make between the 'lost vessel' and the 'victim of manslaughter' in the first half of the sentence, this implied connection making Grandcourt the perpetrator of the crime, and society the indifferent audience of the affair.

Unlike Ruskin and Elizabeth Barrett Browning, George Eliot chooses to expand the issue of the 'fallen woman' to expose the wider implications of social hypocrisy. She uses a narrative tone and language to condemn a society which condones a man's privilege and power and consigns a woman to oblivion. The reader here cannot account for the 'fallen woman' solely with reference to her personal moral character, nor to characteristics of her sex as a whole, but must recognize that society itself is morally implicated in her fate.

These extracts and discussions have provided only a brief glimpse of the wealth of Victorian literature which deals with what was referred to as the 'woman question'; that is, the endless debate on women's proper role in that society. Our intention has not been to offer you a full range of those views, but to highlight some of the main aspects widely held to belong to the ideal woman. We have also seen how the nature of those attitudes and their implications is to be discovered through careful analysis of the tone, the images and arguments which shape them. Elizabeth Barrett Browning's poem and the extract from George Eliot's *Daniel Deronda* indicate how Victorians also looked critically at their own attitudes and recognized some of the problems inherent in the double standards by which men and women were expected to act and by which their actions were judged.

4.4 RELIGION AND ATTITUDES TO WOMEN

The preceding discussion of literary representations of women and their role has stressed that even some Victorian writers critical of prevailing assumptions about women tended in the end to see a woman as determined by her potential as a mother. It also shows, in the discussion of Ruskin's 'Of Queens' Gardens', how women and men were held to occupy separate spheres each appropriate to their differing natural abilities. Men were to participate in the public sphere, in the open world; women were to cultivate the domestic, private sphere, protected from temptation and danger, and sustaining and nurturing the moral values which men must put at risk in their involvement with the wider, public world. The home which the woman creates is, according to Ruskin, to be a shelter from injury, terror, doubt and division.

Ruskin's prose is, as you have seen, shot through with religious imagery and language; but it is not in itself a piece of religious writing. On the other hand, the sermon by H. P. Liddon which you read earlier is a specifically religious text.

Exercise

Re-read paragraph 2 of Liddon's sermon (extract III.8 in the Course Reader)

1 In what ways does Liddon agree with Ruskin's views on the role of women?
2 Do you think that Liddon adds a specifically religious dimension to the role of women?

Specimen answer and discussion

1 Liddon agrees with Ruskin in his assumption that the home is the centre and source of kindliness, courtesy and refinement, in which the finer side of human life and nature is cultivated. It is, moreover, the wife and mother who is to nurture and sustain these qualities. The man will 'escape' to home after the day's 'toil and rivalry' in public life and he will know that at home he will be interpreted generously. The mother, Liddon remarks, 'should be a presiding genius of kindliness and cleanliness'. Implicitly, Liddon and Ruskin are also in agreement that this ideal of womanhood is actually an ideal for the middle-class woman. Neither writer states this clearly but it is implicit in both, for the ideal envisages the woman as wife, mother and home-maker, not a wage earner. Yet, as Best amply illustrates in his section on women and the 'making of livings', the reality for most working-class women was employment in some form of industry or domestic service. Liddon does acknowledge that poverty and living conditions may prevent the realization of this ideal in working-class homes, but he does not explicitly acknowledge the need for women in working-class communities to become wage earners. Ruskin, Liddon and the majority of Victorian social commentators held an ideal of woman that was emphatically a middle-class ideal.

2 Apart from the remark that poverty often blights the domestic happiness which prepares the way of religion in the soul I do not think Liddon's remarks add a specifically religious content to the ideal of womanhood which he advocates. The context of Liddon's remarks, namely that of a sermon, is clearly religious, and he clearly considers the ideal to have religious implications, but I think the specific content of the ideal of womanhood here put forward could just as easily come from a secular source. Does this therefore mean that Victorian religion *simply* echoed the values of its secular contemporaries in respect of women? That would be a rather simplistic view of the relationship between Victorian religion and social values. What Liddon's sermon shows is that religious and secular influences on social values were interwoven in a way that makes them hard to disentangle.

In fact, Victorian religion both contributed its own dimension to the prevailing ideal of womanhood and also sanctified elements of that ideal which originated from secular thought and influences. The evangelical tradition had made the reform of public and private morality one of its main concerns, and the home and family were, in turn, the centre and focus of evangelical morality. It has been said that evangelicalism was above all else the religion of the home. In addition, evangelicalism – and also much of the High Church tradition – advocated a literal and uncritical understanding of the Bible. They thus took literally passages which spoke of the need for women to be subservient or obedient to men.

Confronted with an era of rapid urbanization and industrialization, in which social upheaval had shaken many aspects of traditional social and family life, and also confronted by intellectual and moral challenges to many traditional Christian beliefs, the home became, for traditional Victorian believers, the vital bastion against infidelity, doubt and secularity. The wife and mother accordingly became the guardian of those moral and religious values and beliefs which were so threatened and challenged elsewhere in the public sphere of Victorian Britain.

Thus Victorian religion helped define the dominant ideal of womanhood. On the one hand it reinforced the moral role of women by adding the religious motive and justification to the arguments from nature, biology, law and instinct. On the other hand it added to the role of moral guardian the role of spiritual guardian, guardian of the spiritual life of home, of family, and especially of children.

There were, of course, alternative views of women, of their role and status within the religious community as well as beyond it. Indeed, a significant number of the women who actively campaigned for reforms in the law concerning women, for extension of women's education and for the broadening of opportunities and rights of women generally in Victorian society, were themselves practising Christians. Moreover, it is one of the ironies of the dominant ideal of womanhood which we have examined that experience of philanthropic and charitable work – which was one of the few public activities which the ideal approved for women – frequently led women to seek broader and more public opportunities. These, however, were the exception not the rule: the major contribution of religion to the Victorian view of the role and status of women was to massively support the prevailing ideal of separate spheres.

5 CRITICS OF THE VICTORIAN SOCIAL ORDER

Geoffrey Best, in *Mid-Victorian Britain* 1851–75, attaches considerable importance to the role of what he terms a 'social value system' in preserving the social order in the years 1851–70. Towards the end of this period, he notes (see especially pp. 306 ff.), there were a number of changes. In particular, from our point of view, there was a breakdown in the consensus over social values that had prevailed during the mid-Victorian period. Best's view is that whereas the mid-Victorian calm was scarcely ruffled by dissent, social criticism later became both more radical and more influential.

We have already seen some reason to qualify Best's account. Ideas other than those which have been claimed to be the 'dominant ideology' were seriously canvassed – for instance, by the followers of Thomas Carlyle (e.g. see Sections 3.1 and 3.2 above). But it might be said that these stopped short of being positively subversive insofar as they did not challenge the social hierarchy and the consequential division of British society into 'haves' and 'have-nots'. This is not to say that the problems of the poor were regarded with indifference. Dickens called for greater imagination and sympathy. And churchmen like Liddon (see Section 3.3 above) called increasingly for a 'wise philanthropy' and better legislation to improve the lot of the poor. By and large, however, these were appeals to the consciences of the better-off to do things on behalf of the poorest members of their society. 'Charity' was not yet a dirty word.

But even during the mid-Victorian period there were those who called in question the very social order that made this kind of charity necessary. There was criticism of profit making from 'socialists' who wished to see the means of acquiring wealth removed from individuals and vested instead in the state or in cooperatives. There were even those who wished to see private property abolished altogether. These last were known as 'communists', but we must remember that the political vocabulary of the nineteenth century, although it might seem familiar – 'conservative', 'liberal', 'socialist', 'communist' and even 'social democrat' were all words in use – should not be understood in twentieth-century terms. In particular, it is worth noting that what were called 'socialist' and 'communist' ideas were already familiar to those who read the social criticism of the period long before Karl Marx's ideas made any impact. The social critics we shall be considering are all men whose writings had an influence during our period. In Marx's case, however, that influence was only beginning to be widely felt in the last decades of the century. In each case we shall consider how well the critic fits into the picture presented by Best.

5.1 JOHN STUART MILL AND 'REMOVABLE INEQUALITIES'

According to Professor Best there were no social critics in the mid-Victorian period who were both influential and genuinely radical (see Best, p. 289). He does not discuss the case of John Stuart Mill. Yet, on the face of it, Mill's claim to be thought of as an influential radical is a strong one. His *Principles of Political Economy* and his essays *On Liberty* and *Representative Government* sold in large numbers in cheap 'People's Editions'. His name became well enough known to get him elected to Parliament in 1865 without his engaging in any of the doubtful electoral practices that were then common. Although he himself was strongly in favour of allowing public meetings in London's parks he intervened on one occasion (successfully) to persuade leaders of the radical Reform League to cancel a meeting in Hyde Park which would have led to a serious confrontation with the military. Although his amendment to the Reform Bill, proposing the extension of the suffrage to women on the same basis as men, was lost, it attracted much more support than was expected.

There is little doubt that Mill saw himself as a radical and that he sought to be an influential one. He was no defender of 'respectability' insofar as that involved conforming to the precepts of established religion. The practice of 'deference' belonged, as he saw it, to a paternalistic arrangement of society which he explicitly criticized (this is discussed further in Unit 27). A religious morality might allow that, while all men are equal in the sight of God, it was natural or at least inevitable that human societies would be unequal. But Mill's moral philosophy cannot allow this. In his essay *Utilitarianism* he remarks that the Greatest Happiness Principle 'is a mere form of words, unless one person's happiness . . . is counted for exactly as much as another's' (Everyman edition, p. 58). He quotes with favour the dictum of his mentor Jeremy Bentham: 'everyone to count for one, nobody for more than one'. On this view, as Mill goes on to acknowledge, social inequalities could only be justified as necessary but temporary expedients, as part of a phase a society has to go through in order to reach a stage in which the equal claim of everybody to the means of happiness can be honoured in practice.

Mill himself saw that a 'removable inequalities' theory, such as could be offered on this basis, might take the form of special pleading for the extension of privileges for some at the expense of others. He implies, in *Utilitarianism,* that just such special pleading was involved in his own time in defence of 'the aristocracies of colour, race, and sex' (p. 59). Mill's *Subjection of Women* is an attempt to show that no reasonable case can be made for denying women equality of treatment with men. But Mill did not deny that certain social inequalities might be defended as necessary though temporary expedients. As we shall see, he thought it was possible to defend an unequal distribution of wealth on just this basis.

It is Mill's defence of private property, including its unequal distribution, which marks him out as a defender of 'removable inequalities'. But there are important differences between what Mill defended, and what was defended by Smiles and Palmerston. In the first place, Mill was not arguing, as they were, that it is possible for individuals to raise themselves and hence that the inequalities were removable *for them* even though society would remain hierarchical. Mill's intention, by contrast, was to argue that his own society, in spite of its glaring evils, provided a better basis than other societies for development towards a society in which each person had equal access to the means of happiness. His disagreement with radicals like the French Communist François Fourier (1772–1837) was (as he saw it) primarily one about means rather than ends. He would have strenuously denied the charge that he was trying to defend the interests of a privileged minority and therefore to perpetuate an unequal society. He saw himself, therefore, as a genuine radical, with an open mind about radical alternatives to the society he knew. In his *Principles of Political Economy* he devoted a good deal of attention to these alternatives.

Mill on alternative forms of society

In the eyes of the 'communists' the root of the evils of early nineteenth-century European society was private property. The emphasis of the 'socialists', on the other hand, was on the abolition of competition. Mill accepted that his own society tended to promote morally undesirable characteristics in its members and that it tended to discourage sympathy, charity or human brotherhood. He shared some of the idealism of the communists and the socialists even though, as we shall see, he did not arrive at the same conclusions.

Private property and communism

In his *Principles of Political Economy* Mill addressed himself to the merits and disadvantages of societies organized on communist lines, with private property abolished. I suggest you read the extract from the chapter on property (extract III. 10 (a) in the Course Reader). When you have done so, make a note of your answers to the following questions.

Exercise

1 Did Mill think that a communist society would be better than the one in which he lived?

2 What, for Mill, are the drawbacks of communist societies?

3 Do you think that Mill comes down in the end in favour of a society in which there is private property in some form? Or does he suspend judgement as to whether such a society would be better than a communist one?

Specimen answers

1 Yes. Mill says that if the choice were straightforwardly one between communism and 'the present state of society with all its sufferings and injustices', objections to communism would be 'but as dust in the balance' (paragraph 12).

2 Mill suspends judgement on the common objection that communism would reduce the incentive to work. As to the 'selfish intemperance' of having too many

children, communism would be more likely to reduce this evil than increase it. A 'more real difficulty' faced by communism, according to Mill, would be in distributing work fairly and effectively. But perhaps the most serious difficulty is that public opinion in communist society would need to exercise a great restraint on individual behaviour and that it might become a 'tyrannical yoke', stifling individuality.

3   Mill does not regard any of the objections he mentions as conclusive. Not enough trial had been made of forming communist societies to judge whether these are insuperable objections to that way of organizing society. At the same time Mill is evidently inclined to think that public opinion in communistic societies would be even more oppressive than in mid-Victorian Britain, since the individual would be even more dependent on the mass.

Discussion

It is difficult not to be struck by the strong language with which Mill concludes the extract we have just been studying. He evidently felt that Victorian society tended to grind down individuals 'into a tame uniformity of thoughts and feelings', that this was one of its 'glaring evils'. What Mill refers to as 'individuality of character' is evidently very high amongst his social values. What he calls 'personal and mental freedom' is much more important to Mill than the so-called 'economic' freedoms. He does not even mention the objection that a communist society would deprive individuals of the right to choose their employment. Mill's objection to everyone taking their turn at different kinds of work is only that this would be less productive than if they were specialized. He does not mention that a loss of freedom would be involved.

Mill is in fact very generous, not only in his treatment of communism, but of radical alternatives to existing society generally. This is partly because he thought his own society left much to be desired. At the same time he was far from thinking that any change would, in the long run, necessarily be an improvement. What he wanted to see were experiments in various kinds of community life which could be analysed so that the potentialities of human nature could be reasonably assessed. He rejected the view that, on the basis of studying known societies, we could conclude that human beings are naturally selfish and that society should be organized so as to make it in people's interests to act for the public good. 'Mankind', he declares roundly in the passage we have just studied, 'are capable of a far greater amount of public spirit than the present age is accustomed to suppose possible'. Communist societies might foster this capacity just as 'the existing social institutions', according to Mill, fostered 'the selfish type of character' (Mill, *Principles*, p. 362).

The co-operative movement

Among the experiments in social organization which Mill particularly favoured were those of the co-operative movement in industry, which had been growing in the mid-nineteenth century, both in Britain and in France. Mill wrote at some length about co-operatives in a chapter of his *Principles* entitled 'Of the Probable Future of the Labouring Classes'. You will find his concluding assessment of the prospects for the co-operative movement in extract III. 10 (c) in the Course Reader. You should read that assessment now.

Exercise

1   On what grounds does Mill base his optimism about the future of co-operatives?
2   Do you think his optimism was justified?

Discussion

1   Mill admits that, in the short run, businesses run by a collective management

were at a disadvantage in competition with those run by individuals whose capital is at stake. His optimism is based on his expectation that, as co-operative societies multiply, workpeople will increasingly refuse to work except where they are able to share in the profits. It would then gradually become to the advantage of owners of capital to invest in the co-operatives rather than attempt to maintain 'the old system'.

2   I don't think that Mill was justified in his optimism. He simply *assumes* that there will come a point at which 'co-operative societies shall have sufficiently multiplied' so as to put 'the old system' at a disadvantage in the competition for labour. But it is not clear *how* this breakthrough point would ever be reached.

Mill seems to me to have been guilty of wishful thinking. In his final paragraph he seems to be describing a utopia. I was struck particularly by this sentence:

> Eventually, and in perhaps a less remote future than may be supposed, we may, through the co-operative principle, see our way to a change in society, which could combine the freedom and independence of the individual, with the moral, intellectual, and economical advantages of aggregate production; and which, without violence or spoliation, or even a sudden disturbance of existing habits and expectations, would realise, at least in the industrial department, the best aspirations of the democratic spirit, by putting an end to the division of society into the industrious and the idle, and effacing all social distinctions but those fairly earned by personal services and exertions.

These are fine sentiments, no doubt, but Mill was not justified in believing that such a society would even be achieved eventually or that it could be achieved 'without violence or spoliation, or even a sudden disturbance of existing habits and expectations'. If that is a fair assessment of Mill then it raises a question: why, if Mill was prepared to be radical about the ends, about the kind of society he wanted to see happen, was he not prepared to be radical about the means? What would be wrong about disturbing existing habits and expectations in a society as full of 'glaring evils' as Mill believed his own society was?

I think the answer may lie in two fundamental attitudes which Mill shared with many other Victorians. One is a conviction that revolutions are merely destructive. The other is a belief in the eventual triumph of 'progressive' ideas and therefore in the tendency of society to gradual improvement. In some respects this latter idea seems surprisingly naïve. Not only have co-operatives not become an important sector of industry but there was never any good reason to suppose that they would. To be fair to Mill, however, he was quite right in seeing the labouring classes as an increasingly important part of an industrial society and in foreseeing that their demands would ensure that society would become at least more equal than it had been.

Socialism and individual initiative

We have seen that Mill believed, in opposition to the communists, in the retention of private property. On the other hand he wanted to see a more equal society such as that promoted by co-operative ownership of industry. In these respects, at least, he had much in common with the socialists. Mill took it to be the central feature of socialism to promote a society in which 'not only the instruments of production, the land and the capital, are the joint property of the community, but the produce is divided and the labour apportioned, as far as possible, equally' (Mill, *Principles*, pp. 361ff).

In his chapter on 'The Probable Future of the Labouring Classes' (Course Reader, extract III. 10(d)), Mill gave a brief account of where he stood in relation to socialism.

Exercise

You should read that section now and make a note of why Mill did not regard himself as a socialist.

Discussion

Mill thought competition could be socially valuable in 'discouraging a natural tendency to want to be protected in idleness' and in encouraging a 'spirit of individual exertion'. Human beings require activity, Mill thought, in order to develop their individual potential. Otherwise they deteriorate.

Mill and mid-Victorian ideology

Mill's statement that every restriction of competition is 'an evil, and every extension of it... is always an ultimate good' shows him to be in broad agreement with economic liberalism. According to this view (sometimes referred to as the policy of *laissez-faire*) a government should remove all obstacles to competition and individual enterprise. It would be inconsistent with this view for a government to encourage co-operatives at the expense of the capitalist sector of industry by subsidies or other means. But Mill did not adhere to *laissez-faire* (literally 'leave to do') in an unqualified way, as is clear in another passage from his *Principles of Political Economy*:

> It is... necessary to add, that the intervention of government cannot always practically stop short at the limit which defines the cases intrinsically suitable for it. In the particular circumstances of a given age or nation, there is scarcely anything, really important to the general interest, which it may not be desirable, or even necessary, that the government should take upon itself, not because private individuals cannot effectually perform it, but because they will not. At some times and places there will be no roads, docks, harbours, canals, works of irrigation, hospitals, schools, colleges, printing presses, unless the government establishes them: the public being either too poor to command the necessary resources, or too little advanced in intelligence to appreciate the ends, or not sufficiently practised in joint action to be capable of the means. (Mill, *Principles*, pp. 345ff.)

These principles indicate the kind of intervention in the economy which Mill thought might be necessary on the part of a government. Had he been aware that there was no prospect of the co-operative movement succeeding he could, consistently with such principles, have advocated the granting of public loans to enable them to get under way. The fact that he did not do this might be explained in one of two ways. Either (a) he genuinely believed that such measures would be uncalled for (since co-operatives would multiply and flourish anyway) or else (b) he did not really regard the success of co-operatives as sufficiently 'important to the general interest'. These represent two possible interpretations of Mill's social philosophy. If (b) is true, then Mill can be seen as an advocate of the dominant ideology, as someone not genuinely concerned to abolish inequalities but content to offer the pious hope that they may one day be 'removable'. If, on the other hand, (a) is true, then there is a case for regarding Mill as an exception to Best's claim that there were no radical critics of the mid-Victorian social order who had any influence.

Something can be said for each of these interpretations. Mill's attitude to conventional mid-Victorian social values was not one of either total acceptance or total rejection. On the one hand his dislike of social hierarchy seems to have been genuine. But he was clearly committed to virtues like independence, self-help, individual exertion and to the corresponding social philosophy of *laissez-faire*. Mill did not wish to see the existing social order overturned because it provided a framework within which liberty and individuality might flourish. But he did not think that mid-Victorian society was at all liberal in respecting individuality. Indeed, it seems clear that he was a rebel against the conformist and paternalistic aspects of his own society which Best partially labels by talking of 'respectability' and 'deference'.

The form of 'removable inequalities' theory implicit in the writings of Samuel Smiles exaggerates the extent to which there was, in mid-Victorian Britain, equality of opportunity. Mill was, at least in the case of women, quite clear that such equality did not exist and had to be fought for. Moreover, in his utopia, there would be an end to 'all social distinctions but those fairly earned by personal services and exertions'. Mill's support for the existing order of society seems, therefore, to have been for his own reasons and not because he believed in privilege or social hierarchy.

On balance, therefore, I think that Mill's social philosophy is a significant departure from what Best represents as the prevailing ideology of the mid-Victorian period and that he looked forward to a very different social order from that in which he lived. It may be, then, that Best has exaggerated the extent to which the relative stability of the mid-Victorian period is due to people's sharing the same ideas. It may be that, whatever their ideas, people felt able to be optimistic about what the existing social order could offer them and those they cared about in a way in which they could not subsequently be to the same extent. At all events Mill, as we have seen, was optimistic. As to what he might have thought, had he lived beyond the mid-Victorian period, we cannot of course know. Mill died in 1873.

5.2 KARL MARX

Karl Marx lived in exile (from his native Germany) in London from 1849 till his death in 1883. During that time he researched and wrote the work *Das Kapital* on which his reputation as the great theoretician of modern communism above all rests. In this book he sought to argue that there were forces at work which would lead to the eventual destruction of existing ('capitalist') society. *Das Kapital* was unfinished at Marx's death but completed by his close friend and patron Friedrich Engels. Marx himself was able to see the publication of only the first volume in 1867. (It was published in German. The first English edition did not appear until 1887.) It was reviewed in one or two places. But the extent of Marx's obscurity in Victorian Britain is captured in a chance remark by his reviewer in *The Saturday Review*: '... his [Marx's] facts and illustrations are chiefly drawn from the social circumstances of England where he appears to have resided for some years'.

At least by 1868 Marx seems to have acquired no local reputation in England of any kind. There is no evidence that Mill had even heard of him. But this was not because Marx was not involved actively in promoting the communist cause. He was a dominant influence in the International Workingmen's Association. Exaggerated accounts were reported of that body's involvement in the events of the Paris Commune, as a result of which Marx achieved a brief notoriety in the early 1870s as 'the Red Terror Doctor'. But there seems little reason to object to the assessment by the relatively sympathetic John Rae, who wrote in the *Contemporary Review* for 1881 that

> the country where [Marx] is least known is that in which he has for the last 30 years lived and worked... the writings of Marx are hardly better known in this country than those of Confucius and it is doubtful whether, outside of a few Radical clubs in London, the English proletariat so much as know his name.

It is likely, however, that Marx's ideas were better known than this assessment implies. *The Communist Manifesto* of 1848, which he and Engels had drafted, was widely circulated and provoked a strong reaction from *The Times* editorial of 2 September 1851. The editorial fastened on passages that envisaged the abolition of private property and ('bourgeois') marriage. Briefly, and anonymously, Marx was to fall into the category of mid-Victorian social critics who were, in Best's phrase, 'deplored and ignored' (Best, p. 289). The editorial concludes on a note at once magisterial and dismissive:

> These are but slight specimens of this Literature for the Poor; yet we think they will suffice to excite attention for the only legitimate means by which this great evil can be counteracted. Let a provident spirit of conciliation enable the wise and the good to offer to the people a beneficial education in place of this abominable teaching.

It is clear enough that *The Times* regarded it as 'abominable' to suggest the abolition of private property and marriage. It is clear also that poverty ('this great evil') was a problem which required 'a spirit of conciliation'. Whether the 'beneficial education' referred to would involve what Best refers to as the idea of 'removable inequalities' is not clear. But it might very well have done. Poverty is a 'great evil' but one that 'can be counteracted' according to the editorial. Yet it is not clear what the 'legitimate' means of avoiding it would have been, if not the then much-vaunted remedy of hard work on the part of the poor themselves. The 'beneficial education' might then be that offered by the likes of Samuel Smiles, an education in the virtues of self-help. That would be an 'education' (or better, an 'induction') into what was earlier (see Section 2.1 above) referred to as the 'dominant ideology'.

The theory that the value system that prevails in a given society reflects the interests of the dominant class is one of Marx's most original contributions to social thought. The analysis I have just given of *The Times* editorial is one a Marxist could accept. But there would be nothing at all profound about seeing that a *Times* editorial of 1851 was championing the interests of the propertied classes. Marx's own analysis was directed at revealing ideological content where it was by no means so easy to detect, in particular in the supposed 'science' of political economy.

Marx was particularly struck by an assumption which had pervaded the British tradition of political economy from Adam Smith (1723–90) to John Stuart Mill. It was that a society was no more than a collection of individuals, bound together only by considerations of mutual self-interest. The helplessness of each individual was off-set by the human capacity to make a bargain. Economic life was thus the most basic form of human social life. As Adam Smith had put it, in his *The Wealth of Nations* (1776):

> In almost every other race of animals each individual, when it is grown up to maturity, is entirely independent, and in its natural state has occasion for the assistance of no other living creature. But man has almost constant occasion for the help of his brethren, and it is in vain for him to expect it from their benevolence only. He will be more likely to prevail if he can interest their self-love in his favour, and show them that it is for their own advantage to do for him what he requires of them. Whoever offers to another a bargain of any kind, proposes to do this. Give me that which I want, and you shall have this which you want, is the meaning of every such offer; and it is in this manner that we obtain from one another the far greater part of those good offices which we stand in need of. It is not from the benevolence of the butcher, the brewer, or the baker that we expect our dinner, but from their regard to their own interest. We address ourselves, not to their humanity but to their self-love, and never talk to them of our own necessities but of their advantages. (Adam Smith, *The Wealth of Nations*, pp. 118ff.)

Marx was in many ways indebted to the British tradition of political economy. But he took exception to this assumption about social life as founded on contracts between individuals. That view of the isolated individual who enters society for what he can get out of it was, according to Marx, the product of historical developments that had taken place in the seventeenth and eighteenth centuries and not a timeless fact of human nature. In his *Grundrisse* – a draft of his critique of political economy – Marx began by insisting on this point:

> The more deeply we go back into history, the more does the individual, and hence also the producing individual, appear as a dependent, as belonging to a greater whole: in a still quite natural way in the family and in the family expanded into the clan; then later in the various forms of communal society arising out of the antitheses and fusions of the clans. Only in the eighteenth century, in 'civil society', do the various forms of social connectedness confront the individual as a mere means towards his private purpose, as external necessity. (Marx, *Grundrisse*, p. 84).

Marx went on to accuse the political economists of quietly smuggling in commercial middle-class relationships as if they were the natural and unalterable basis for any society at any time. But, according to Marx, there is no such thing as human nature or society considered in abstraction from particular historical processes. Political economy simply presented the relations of a capitalist phase of human society in the idealized form of an abstract theory. On his analysis it contained a middle-class ideology at its very foundations. Those who believed that political economy was a timeless science of human nature and society in the abstract, which propounded 'eternal natural laws' (*Grundrisse*, p. 87), were engaged in deception – both of themselves and of those who invoked the authority of political economy in advocating what they claimed was the right order of society. They were, in effect, engaging in ideology.

'Ideology', as Marx used the term, has the appearance of objective fact but its purpose is to serve the interests of one class over and against those of another. It involves a kind of self-deception on the part of those who produce it. Marx's collaborator Friedrich Engels gave this explanation:

> Ideology is a process accomplished by the so-called thinker consciously indeed but with a false consciousness. The real motives impelling him remain unknown to him, otherwise it would be not an ideological process at all. Hence he imagines false or apparent motives.

The economist who postulates a natural state in which independent individuals associate with one another only on the basis of a contract will at one level think he is contributing to scientific knowledge. He will say he is trying to understand how society works, how wealth is created, and so on. But in reality, according to Marx, his motives are quite different. His motives are to license, on the one hand, the pursuit of self-interest and in particular the accumulation of individual wealth, and, on the other hand, the rejection of all obligations to others except those arising from something like a contract.

Marx himself had little influence in Britain during our period, as we have seen. His theory of ideology was not appreciated until much later. But the tide was already turning, even in Mill's lifetime, against the dominant individualism of the mid-Victorian period. Mill's later enthusiasm for the co-operative movement may be taken as one sign of this change. By the 1880s socialist ideas had gained a good deal of ground and by the time the first volume of Marx's *Das Kapital* appeared in English in 1887 there was a much more receptive readership waiting for it than there had been for the German edition twenty years before. British socialism had a number of roots, some of which you will be reading about in the next section; but it was not originally indebted to the thought of Karl Marx.

5.3 F. D. MAURICE AND CHRISTIAN SOCIALISM

One of the points which emerges from our consideration of religion and social values is that a particular set of influences – in this case those arising from religion – can simultaneously support the dominant values of a society and also nurture rather different values. We saw that Victorian religious life gave support to the dominant attitudes to work, poverty, respectability and social hierarchy (Section 3.3) as well as those towards the place of women (Section 4.4). At the same time Christian ideas could be, and were, taken to point towards quite different attitudes, emphasizing co-operation rather than competition and a concern for others rather than a narrow pursuit of self-help.

One of the more striking examples of this more critical role of religion was the movement known as 'Christian Socialism', which came to the fore between 1848 and 1854. Perhaps the most influential, though not the most radical, leader of the Christian Socialists was Frederick Denison Maurice (1805–72). Maurice, an Anglican clergyman of 'Broad' or 'liberal' theological views, seems to have coined the phrase 'Christian Socialism' when he and a circle of like-minded people set about writing 'tracts' to make their position clear to the public at large. He insisted that the title *Tracts on Christian Socialism* was 'the only title which will define our object, and will commit us at once to the conflict we must engage in sooner or later with the unsocial Christians and the unchristian Socialists'. (Frederick Maurice (ed.), *The Life of Frederick Denison Maurice chiefly told in his own letters,* 2nd edn, Vol. II, pp. 34ff.)

The 'unsocial Christians' were those who were indifferent to the conditions of the working poor and who failed to see that a true socialism was a necessary implication of Christianity. The 'unchristian Socialists', on the other hand, were those who tried to pursue socialist values in a purely secular way. Christianity, Maurice insisted, was the only foundation of socialism:

> Peaceful co-operation, a living brotherhood of fellow-workers, demands the recognition of a great elder brother, who is one with that Invisible Lord, and one with His creatures and servants. A brotherhood to be real demands a Father; therefore it is that we speak of Christian Socialism. (*Tracts by Christian Socialists,* no. III (1850) 'An Address to the Clergy . . .')

For all that Maurice was opposed to competitive individualism and anxious to stress the brotherhood of man, he refused to take up political activity or to associate himself with any political faction. In this respect he was a restraining influence on the Christian Socialists, whom he encouraged rather to engage in social work. Although he in some sense believed that all people are fundamentally equal, because equal in the sight of God, he did not take this as meaning that they should have equal political power. He seems, rather like Dickens, to have been more concerned with there being better conditions for the poor and better relations between people at different levels of the social hierarchy than with challenging the existence of the hierarchy as such.

How then are we to evaluate Best's claim that a mid-Victorian consensus gave way to more radical social criticism by the 1870s? Looking at this from the standpoint of religion and social values it is the ambiguity of the picture which is most striking.

Certainly, as we noted on p. 91, by 1890 the dissenting voices from within the various churches concerning social values were more numerous, more varied and more insistent than they were in 1850. But the most famous of the Christian Socialists, F. D. Maurice, Charles Kingsley and Thomas Hughes, had been at their most prominent and influential in the years 1848–54. Equally importantly, we must not assume that, because dissenting voices increased, the more conservative traditions simply declined. For example, in 1874 a group of prominent Anglican women formed the Girls Friendly Society. It succeeded at once and quickly developed a national and local network of organizations. Its aims were squarely in line with the dominant set of attitudes and values with which we have been concerned. It emphasized the virtues of respectability, home, family and motherhood, and it also stressed the importance of deference, co-operation between social classes and hard work: the 'members' of the Girls Friendly Society were from the working classes and lower middle class, the leaders of the Society were known as 'Associates' and were of middle and upper-class backgrounds. The Associate was, ideally, energetic, devout and an enthusiastic exponent of charity and good works. The member was, ideally, devout, kindly, serious, deferential and hard working.

In the 1880s the Girls Friendly Society was only one of a variety of religious groups and organizations which set out to sustain the older dominant set of values and to resist the dissenting voices. But even here there was ambiguity, for it was by no means unknown for an Associate within the Girls Friendly Society to discover, in her public work for the Society, a taste and ability in public life which worked against the very traditional values which the society sought to uphold.

5.4 JOHN RUSKIN AND WILLIAM MORRIS

In this section, I shall consider John Ruskin and William Morris as critics of the prevailing social order. Ruskin has already been mentioned frequently in these units; Morris has not, but will be discussed further in Units 29–30 and more fully in Units 31–32. So first of all let me sketch out a few details about Morris, whose many-sided career spans our period. He was the son of a wealthy bill-broker – so, like Ruskin, who was the son of a wine shipper, a member of the prosperous middle classes. But Morris was of a younger generation and still at school in 1851, when Ruskin defended the Pre-Raphaelites in *The Times* against adverse criticism of their work. Morris went up to Oxford in 1853, where he met Burne-Jones; they became keen followers of Ruskin, whose reputation as an art critic was already well established. Their interest in, and involvement with, Pre-Raphaelitism also grew, though the original close-knit group of the Pre-Raphaelite Brotherhood had largely disintegrated by the mid-1850s. Morris and Burne-Jones were recruited by Rossetti to paint murals for the Oxford Union in 1857, and became part of what has been seen as a second wave of Pre-Raphaelitism. During the late 50s Morris was not only attempting to gain skills in painting, but also writing poetry, and working on illuminations, carving and embroidery. It was the craft tradition that became increasingly important for Morris, in the firm of 'fine art workmen' Morris, Faulkner and Co. set up in 1861, and in Morris and Company, set up in 1875 (with Morris in full control). Morris became a socialist in the 1880s and wrote a considerable number of polemical articles and lectures. In 1882 he joined the Democratic Federation. When this broke up, Morris was one of the founder members of the Socialist League in 1884.

I will concentrate here on Morris's social criticism of the 1880s, in relation to a critical tradition. Morris shared many of the same emphases in his critique of society as both Carlyle and Ruskin before him – for example, in his approach to work, the idea of a divisive society and his antagonism to the *laissez-faire* system. Carlyle had criticized existing social relationships 'with Cash Payment as the sole nexus' (*Works*, Vol. VI, p. 154). So had Ruskin. And Morris attacked 'the subordination of all capacities to the great end of 'money-making' for oneself or one's master' (Morris, *Useful Work Versus Useless Toil,* p. 617). This was not just an attack on a society that seemed overly preoccupied with money: it was an attack on the economic relations at the heart of that society.

Now let us look at Ruskin's social criticism to see how Morris drew on his ideas. From 1850–3 Ruskin was working on *The Stones of Venice,* his major text on architecture; this included the chapter 'On the Nature of Gothic', which was distributed as a sort of manifesto for the Working Men's College opened in 1854. Ruskin taught and lectured at the college in Red Lion Square, London.

Exercise

Now read this extract from Ruskin's 'The Nature of Gothic': sections 11, 12, 13, 14 and 16, from '. . . And this is what we have to do with all our labourers. . .' (extract IV.4 in the Course Reader). You will return to this text in more detail later in Units 29-30.

Briefly comment on the ways in which Ruskin saw industrial labour as degrading.

Discussion

Ruskin believed that the present system reduced labour to inhuman, mechanical tasks. It is not merely the machine that is blamed for such evils, but a society that can transform its workers into machine-like components for profit, for surplus. This ties up directly with Ruskin's criticism of the Great Exhibition and the Crystal Palace, discussed in Unit 16. You may also have been struck, as I was, by the difference between this text and 'Of Queens' Gardens' (pp. 98–100). The working man's labour is seen in terms of, and relative to, a complex of social and economic relations – as opposed to the absolute terms in which he discussed women.

The nature and quality of work was central to Ruskin's critique: it was the cypher of a society. He saw work as the productive basis of life and unhappiness in work as a violation of a God-given right. Ruskin fiercely criticized contemporary social relations, but the kind of society he advocated was nonetheless deeply hierarchical – a society in which each class and group interacted productively in an organic whole. He was none too keen on social mobility:

> When a man born of an artisan was looked upon as an entirely different species of animal from a man born of a noble, it made him no more uncomfortable or ashamed to remain that different species of animal, than it makes a horse, ashamed to remain a horse, and not to become a giraffe. But now that a man may make money, and rise in the world, and associate himself, unreproached, with people once far above him, not only is the natural discontentedness of humanity developed to an unheard-of extent, whatever a man's position, but it becomes a veritable shame to him to remain in the state he was born in, and everybody thinks it his *duty* to try to be a 'gentleman'.
> (Ruskin, *Pre-Raphaelitism*, p. 9)

Ruskin's point was that manual labour (and trade too) should be a dignified occupation and possess 'gentlemanly' qualities, i.e. dignity, piety, honesty, etc. should not be seen as the exclusive preserve of higher social ranks. And he saw the purpose of the Working Man's College to give working men access to learning and knowledge, not merely to equip them with the means to climb out of their class. Unlike Smiles later, then, he saw no virtue in the idea of 'getting on', though Ruskin found the order of contemporary society a great deal less acceptable than Smiles did. Note that the above quotation comes from *Pre-Raphaelitism* (1851): Ruskin did not see a discussion of social relations as irrelevant to art, but saw art as a branch of work that was integrally related to other areas of social life. We shall return to this point later.

Exercise

Now read the extract from Morris's *Useful work versus Useless Toil* (extract III. 11 in the Course Reader). Here Morris distinguishes between different kinds of work and like Ruskin stresses the idea of pleasure in work as the pre-requisite of a just society.
How does Morris account for the inequality in contemporary social life?

Discussion

Morris's account is based on his understanding of Marx. He saw class conflict as endemic to the capitalist system, in the exploitative relation of labour to capital. The workers, the real producers of the wealth, were kept poor in the interests of the owners of capital.

Morris envisaged the overthrow of that class system. What Ruskin had envisaged was very different: ideally, an extremely hierarchical social order with an élite, aristocratic ruling class. But it was the critical aspects of Ruskin's writing that so influenced Morris and subsequent socialist thought. Indeed, Morris later wrote 'it was through him that I learned to give form to my discontent' ('How I became a Socialist', 1894, Course Reader, extract III. 12). It was socialism that gave Morris his framework.

There was much rhetoric in the writings of both Ruskin and Morris and there is a good deal of idealization of the nature of labour in the mediaeval period. (Look again, for instance, at Ruskin's comments on the cathedral in *The Nature of Gothic*.) But to see Ruskin's or Morris's main concerns as to end machine production and get back to a mediaeval world is not only inaccurate, but misrepresents their points of view. Morris was keen to stress that the machine was not *inherently* evil. For instance, he wrote of 'the wonderful machines which in the hands of just and foreseeing men would have been used to minimize repulsive labour and to give pleasure' (W. Morris, *Art and Socialism*, p. 625). Morris also pointed out that the mediaeval period obviously could not, and should not, be reverted to. Ruskin had made the same point.

There are two critical points here that should be borne in mind:

1 the view that what is produced in society must be in some way expressive of that society;

2   the use of the mediaeval period as a model, as a *means* by which to criticize contemporary society.

As I suggested in Units 18–19, Section 6.1, these points are linked. Ruskin again:

> The art of any country *is the exponent of its social and political virtues*. The art, or general productive and formative energy, of any country, is the exact exponent of its ethical life. You can have noble art only from noble persons, associated under laws fitted to their time and circumstances. (Ruskin, *Lectures on Art*, p. 39)

This idea, that art was inextricably bound to political economy, was central also to Morris's analysis of the state of art under capitalism. He saw the degeneration of art as a result of the division of labour and the split between mental and manual work. Morris's view of art was not confined to the conventional category but included all creative aspects of useful work (see 'The Worker's Share of Art' (1885), Course Reader extract IV. 21, where Morris saw art as 'especially the expression of man's pleasure in the deeds of the present; in his work').

He saw the hierarchical distinction between the 'high' or fine arts and the 'lesser' or popular arts as socially determined by the monopoly of commerce and its interests. Thus his own engagement with the craft tradition, which you will look at in Units 31–32. By his own analysis, Morris's attempt to undermine traditional artistic hierarchies was subject to the contradictions of a middle-class radical working within the existing social order. Morris could not work *outside* society. In order to provide a critique of that social order, he published articles through the available channels for dissenting voices in the socialist press. He also set up his own Kelmscott Press in 1891.

Both Ruskin and Morris opposed the dominant set of beliefs about how society functioned. Both sought alternative explanations to a dominant ideology of an ordered, just, progressive and prosperous society. The problems they raised did not disappear with superficial social improvements. For Ruskin, greater material prosperity made little difference to the fundamental impoverishment he identified; and nor did Morris, writing later on in our period, deny that living standards had risen. Their criticisms had a sharper edge: first, by addressing basic social and economic relationships that had not changed despite superficial improvements, and, secondly, by stressing the cost to the quality of life. The critical practice of both Ruskin and Morris was also subject to the ideological framework in which they worked. And those conditions they identified as stifling constrained what was possible in the practice of art. But note that Morris did not use the term 'ideology'. As Stuart Brown mentioned earlier, 'ideology' became a point of theoretical focus in later developments in Marxism in the twentieth century, when Marx's major text on the issue, *The German Ideology*, became available.

Some commentators have seen Morris and Ruskin as nostalgic for times past, and as hopeless idealists. This, I think, is to edit out the critical nature of their work, and to forget that central to their writing was an attack on the present organization of society. In a single reference, Best suggests that Ruskin was applauded and ignored by his contemporaries. For many, no doubt, this was the case, but the interesting question may be how and why such a critique could be so absorbed. Such a simple dismissal is indicative of the fact that Best does not address the issue of a critical culture, nor indeed, the issue of culture generally. It is this issue of culture that you will examine next in Units 22–26.

6 CONCLUDING REMARKS

At the outset we identified three questions as ones we would primarily be concerned to address in this block:

1   How far was there a consensus about moral and social values during our period and to what extent did it begin to disintegrate towards the end?

2   How were subordinate groups like women and poor working people regarded? To what extent were they invited to think of themselves in terms of the same values as others?

3   How far were there alternative sets of values being advocated during our period? How radically different were they? How influential were they?

According to Best and advocates of what we have been calling the 'dominant ideology' thesis there was a high degree of agreement over moral and social values in mid-Victorian Britain (roughly the 1850s and '60s) but less so in the following decades. That agreement centred, according to Best, on ideas of respectability, independence and 'removable inequalities'. There were other values canvassed at the time but these were either not radically different or not very influential at all or not influential until the 1870s or '80s. That is what is contended by advocates of the 'dominant ideology' thesis. The thesis itself is an attempt to explain this supposed fact.

It is useful to ask, what would show the thesis to be false? It would indeed be false if Marx had exercised any significant influence during the mid-Victorian period. For, of the alternative social and moral values we have considered, those of Karl Marx are the most diametrically opposed to the 'dominant ideology'. If any one of those we have considered could be called a 'dissident' it would be Marx. But, as we have seen (Section 5.2 above), Marx was almost unknown in mid-Victorian Britain.

Yet, while we have not found the 'dominant ideology' thesis to be straightforwardly false, we have found reasons for believing that it over-simplifies the moral and social values of mid-Victorian Britain.

Revision exercise

Try to recall some of the respects in which there were alternative moral and social values being put forward in mid-Victorian Britain.

Discussion

None of the social critics we have considered seems to have believed in 'removable inequalities' in the sense explained by Best. Some like Carlyle, Maurice and Dickens accept social hierarchy but call for an understanding sympathy for the conditions of the poor rather than an insistence on their independence. Implicitly or explicitly, such critics reject, as did Ruskin (Section 5.4), a corollary of the 'dominant ideology', namely, that the attitude of government should be one of *laissez-faire*. Others, like Mill (Section 5.1 above), broadly accepted independence and *laissez-faire* but rejected social hierarchy.

Again, although there was something of a consensus about the importance of work, there was a significant deviation from the prevailing view that work is merely instrumental, a means to greater 'independence' and thus 'respectability'. Carlyle's Gospel of Work represents work as important, not for these reasons, but because it is in some way fulfilling (see Section 3.4 above). Carlyle's view of the dignity of labour seems to be that reflected in Brown's painting *Work* and to lead naturally to criticisms such as those of Morris (see Section 5.4) about the kind of work people were expected to do.

Units 20–21 Moral Values and the Social Order

Our study in this block shows that, even if one set of values prevailed during the mid-Victorian period, there was a good deal of at least limited opposition to it. It is true that, of the figures we have considered, only Marx can be held to have been diametrically opposed to the 'dominant ideology'. And Marx, we have conceded, made little impact on the mid-Victorian Britain in which he lived. Morris's more radical socialist writings belong to the last decades of the century. The others, although highly critical of some aspects of the 'dominant ideology', none the less accepted it in other respects. Some opposed the competitive individualism, some the social hierarchy, some the stress on independence and *laissez-faire*. But to the extent that they accepted at least one crucial aspect of the prevailing social order none of Carlyle, Dickens, Mill, Maurice or Ruskin could be called a 'dissident'. To that extent our study broadly confirms the account given by Best.

Where our study points to a particular defect in Best's account is in an assumption he never makes quite explicit and so does not argue for. The assumption is that artistic, religious, literary or philosophical traditions have no life of their own of a kind that might produce a critique of the values which prevail in society at large. It is true that such traditions do in part reflect the values of society at large. But, in varying degree, they can react against them and their reactions can, again in varying degrees, make some difference to what values are prevalent.

The fact that there was a prevailing ideology during the mid-Victorian period does not mean that there was no dissent. On the contrary, there seem to have been a number of variously opposed ideologies. In studying these we have been studying one aspect of the 'culture' of our chosen period. To that extent you should find many points of continuity between your study of this block and your study of the next.

REFERENCES

Best, G. (1979) *Mid-Victorian Britain 1851–75*, Fontana.

Carlyle, T. (1843) *Past and Present*, Chapman and Hall.

Dickens, C. (1854) *Hard Times*, Oxford University Press, 1989.

Ereira, A. (1981) *The People's England*, Routledge and Kegan Paul.

Golby, J. (ed.) (1986) *Culture and Society in Britain 1850–1890: a source book of contemporary writings*, Oxford University Press (referred to in the text as the Course Reader).

Gombrich, E. (1972) 'Action and Expression in Western Art', in Hinde, R. A. (ed.) *Non-verbal Communication*, Cambridge University Press.

Hueffer, F. M. (1896) *Ford Madox Brown: a record of his life and work*, London.

Marx, K. (1867) *Das Kapital*, Vol. 1, Penguin Marx Library.

Marx, K. (written 1857–8; first published 1939) *Grundrisse*, Penguin Marx Library.

Maurice, F. (1884, 2nd edn) *The Life of Frederick Denison Maurice chiefly told in his own letters*, Vol. II, Macmillan.

Mill, J. S. (1848–71) *Principles of Political Economy*, Pelican Classics edn (abridged), 1970.

Mill, J. S. (1859–61) *Utilitarianism, On Liberty and Considerations on Representative Government*, H. B. Acton (ed.) Everyman edn, Dent, 1972.

Mill, J. S. (1869) *On the Subjection of Women*, Longmans.

Morris, W. (1948 edn; first published 1884) 'Art and Socialism', in Cole, G. D. H. (ed.) *William Morris*, Nonesuch Press.

Ruskin, J. (1856) *Modern Painters*, Vol. III (references in text quoted from 2nd edn in small form, George Allen, 1898).

Ruskin, J. (1851) *Pre-Raphaelitism*, London.

Ruskin, J. (1905 edn) 'Lecture on Art', in *The Works of John Ruskin*, Vol. XX, Library Edition.

Smiles, S. (1859) *Self-Help*, many editions.

Smiles, S. (1887) *Life and Labour*, John Murray.

Smith, A. (1776) *The Wealth of Nations*, Pelican Classics edn.

Tracts by Christian Socialists no. III (1850) 'An Address to the Clergy...'